# Swift 2 Design Patterns

Build robust and scalable iOS and Mac OS X game applications

**Julien Lange**

**[PACKT]** open source *
PUBLISHING    community experience distilled

BIRMINGHAM - MUMBAI

# Swift 2 Design Patterns

First published: October 2015

Production reference: 1231015

Published by Packt Publishing Ltd.
Livery Place
35 Livery Street
Birmingham B3 2PB, UK.

ISBN 978-1-78588-761-1

www.packtpub.com

# Credits

**Author**
Julien Lange

**Reviewers**
Vladimir Pouzanov
Victor Sigler
Ye Xiaodong

**Acquisition Editor**
Tushar Gupta

**Content Development Editor**
Shali Deeraj

**Technical Editor**
Saurabh Malhotra

**Copy Editors**
Rashmi Sawant
Sneha Singh

**Project Coordinator**
Kinjal Bari

**Proofreader**
Safis Editing

**Indexer**
Hemangini Bari

**Graphics**
Disha Haria
Jason Monteiro
Abhinash Sahu

**Production Coordinator**
Komal Ramchandani

**Cover Work**
Komal Ramchandani

# About the Author

**Julien Lange** is a 34-year-old IT expert in software engineering. He started developing on an Amstrad CPC464 with the BASIC language when he was 7 years old. He later learned Visual Basic 3/4, then VB.NET, and then C#. For several years until the end of his education, he developed and maintained several e-business websites based on PHP and ASP.NET. After his graduation, he continued to learn more and more about software, which included software architecture and project management, and always tried to acquire new skills. Since 2011, he has been working as an IT project manager on the lead management middleware of DSI Axa France (a French insurance company). This middleware is based on the SOA architecture. As this middleware is consumed by frontend users exposed on the Internet, performance is the top priority each time he delivers a new release of the system. Scalability and robustness are really important in his everyday work.

He first developed an interest in mobile development in 2009. After discovering the massive potential of iPhone games and software, he decided to find an improved game engine, which would allow him to concentrate only on the main purpose of a game: developing a game and not a game engine. His choice was Unity 3D. Later, he took some time to learn the native iOS Objective-C language, which was quite difficult for him due to its language particularity and finally learned Swift since its first apparition in 2014. In addition to his main work as an IT consultant, he created `iXGaming.com` in December 2010. He currently has several projects in mind, including a game based on a French board game and a new website that delivers new services to developers. He is searching for a few partners to work with.

After reviewing several books by Packt Publishing, I decided to write a book for them. I would especially like to thank all the members of Packt Publishing, including Shali, Tushar, and Sam. I would also thank, every reviewer and especially Victor Sigler for their times reviewing this book. Also, I would to thank my family, and most of all my wife, for allowing me to take some time to write this book. I would also like to thank a few people with whom I work everyday: Adrien D, Alain De L, Juliette O., Raphael D, Stephane D, Helmi C, and Christelle P.

# About the Reviewers

**Vladimir Pouzanov** is a systems engineer and embedded enthusiast. He has spent countless hours hacking different mobile hardware, porting Linux to various devices that were not supposed to run it, and toying around outside the iOS sandbox. He has also been a professional iOS consultant and has been developing applications based on iOS ever since the first Apple iPhones became available. Later on, he switched his professional interest to systems engineering and cloud computing, but he still keeps a close eye on the mobile and embedded world.

> I'd like to give credit to my wife for her amazing support when I was working on the review and sharing my attention between her, our daughter, and the book.

**Victor Sigler** is an iOS software engineer with experience of developing consumer and enterprise mobile applications. He loves everything that is related to Apple. He is passionate about Swift and the world of programming contests. He enjoys writing about iOS development on his blog at http://www.vsigler.com and helps people solve their queries on Stack Overflow. He can be found on Twitter at @Vkt0r.

**Ye Xiaodong** is a full-stack software engineer and technical director of zai360.com, an O2O company that provides a recyclables collection service for Chinese family customers on a periodical basis. He has 7 years of application development experience working for start-ups and leading companies across the world on iOS, Android, Windows Phone, Symbian, and Meego. He has developed lots of iOS applications; designed, created, and maintained iOS libraries and Xcode plugins; and contributed to open source projects, as he is passionate about bringing the latest features to applications. He has worked as a technical reviewer for the book *Mastering Swift*, *Packt Publishing*.

# www.PacktPub.com

## Support files, eBooks, discount offers, and more

For support files and downloads related to your book, please visit www.PacktPub.com.

Did you know that Packt offers eBook versions of every book published, with PDF and ePub files available? You can upgrade to the eBook version at www.PacktPub.com and as a print book customer, you are entitled to a discount on the eBook copy. Get in touch with us at service@packtpub.com for more details.

At www.PacktPub.com, you can also read a collection of free technical articles, sign up for a range of free newsletters and receive exclusive discounts and offers on Packt books and eBooks.

https://www2.packtpub.com/books/subscription/packtlib

Do you need instant solutions to your IT questions? PacktLib is Packt's online digital book library. Here, you can search, access, and read Packt's entire library of books.

## Why subscribe?

- Fully searchable across every book published by Packt
- Copy and paste, print, and bookmark content
- On demand and accessible via a web browser

## Free access for Packt account holders

If you have an account with Packt at www.PacktPub.com, you can use this to access PacktLib today and view 9 entirely free books. Simply use your login credentials for immediate access.

# Table of Contents

# Preface

This book will help you understand when and how to implement the 23 patterns, as described by the gang of four (GoF), with the new language provided by Apple: Swift.

The main idea behind this book is to make it a reference book for implementing a specific pattern. This is the reason why I have divided this book into three categories: creational, structural, and behavioral patterns. For each category, you will find a chapter with a common structure: roles, a UML class diagram, participants, collaboration, illustration, and implementation with Swift.

This structure is an easy way to find the answers that you may ask yourself. In this book, I will first introduce you to the five creational patterns, followed by seven structural patterns, and then conclude with the eleven behavioral patterns, as defined by the GoF.

## What this book covers

*Chapter 1, Creational Patterns,* introduces you to the five patterns of a creational pattern category: the prototype, factory method, singleton, abstract factory, and builder patterns.

*Chapter 2, Structural Patterns – Decorator, Proxy, and Bridge,* introduces you to structural patterns and helps you explore the decorator, proxy, and bridge patterns.

*Chapter 3, Structural Patterns – Composite and Flyweight,* teaches you how to deal with the structure of multiple objects using the composite and flyweight patterns.

*Chapter 4, Structural Patterns – Adapter and Facade,* teaches you how to join the two types that were not designed to work with each other together, thanks to the adapter pattern. Then, you'll learn how the facade pattern can help you simplify the interface of a set of complex systems.

*Chapter 5, Behavioral Patterns – Strategy, State, and Template Method*, introduces you to the behavioral patterns. In this chapter, we will discuss the strategy, state, and template method patterns.

*Chapter 6, Behavioral Patterns – Chain of Responsibility and Command*, introduces you to two other behavioral patterns that are concerned with passing requests to an appropriate object that will then execute the action.

*Chapter 7, Behavioral Patterns – Iterator, Mediator, and Observer*, provides a way to implement communication between objects while keeping their independence and anonymity.

*Chapter 8, Behavioral Patterns – Visitor, Interpreter, and Memento*, concludes with the discovery and implementation of the 23 patterns, as defined by the GoF.

# What you need for this book

The only requirement for this book is to have Xcode 7 installed on your Mac computer. All the code provided has been written, compiled, and tested with Swift 2. You don't need any other software to follow the examples provided in this book. All samples in these book have been written using a OSX Command line tool project or a Playground file.

# Who this book is for

This book is intended for beginners as well as senior developers who want to take the next step in the software engineering industry.

This book will help you learn about the difference between a low-level programmer and a programmer with design pattern knowledge. You can apply this knowledge with Swift in Xcode to design scalable and flexible apps or games for iOS and Mac. As design patterns are not the exclusive reserve of Swift, but can be used by any other language, this is the knowledge that any developer and software architect must have.

# Conventions

In this book, you will find a number of text styles that distinguish between different kinds of information. Here are some examples of these styles and an explanation of their meaning.

Code words in text as are shown as follows: "`AbstractExpression`: It defines an `interpret()` method that is common to all node in the abstract syntax tree."

A block of code is set as follows:

```
class WalkMoveStrategy:IMoveStrategy{
  func performMove() {
    print("I am walking")
  }
}
```

When we wish to draw your attention to a particular part of a code block, the relevant lines or items are set in bold:

```
class WalkMoveStrategy:IMoveStrategy{
  func performMove() {
    print("I am walking")
  }
}
```

Any console output is written as follows:

```
Printing checkPoint....
Level: 0    Weapon: gun    Points: 1200
Level: 1    Weapon: tommy gun    Points: 2250
Level: 2    Weapon: bazooka    Points: 2400
Level: 4    Weapon: knife    Points: 3000
Total Points: 8850
```

**New terms** and **important words** are shown in bold. Words that you see on the screen, for example, in menus or dialog boxes, appear in the text like this: "Click on the **Show the Test navigator** button on the left-hand side."

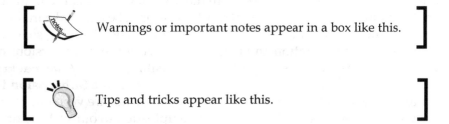

> Warnings or important notes appear in a box like this.

> Tips and tricks appear like this.

# Reader feedback

Feedback from our readers is always welcome. Let us know what you think about this book—what you liked or disliked. Reader feedback is important for us as it helps us develop titles that you will really get the most out of.

To send us general feedback, simply e-mail feedback@packtpub.com, and mention the book's title in the subject of your message.

If there is a topic that you have expertise in and you are interested in either writing or contributing to a book, see our author guide at www.packtpub.com/authors.

# Customer support

Now that you are the proud owner of a Packt book, we have a number of things to help you to get the most from your purchase.

# Downloading the example code

You can download the example code files from your account at http://www.packtpub.com for all the Packt Publishing books you have purchased. If you purchased this book elsewhere, you can visit http://www.packtpub.com/support and register to have the files e-mailed directly to you.

# Downloading the color images of this book

We also provide you with a PDF file that has color images of the screenshots/diagrams used in this book. The color images will help you better understand the changes in the output. You can download this file from http://www.packtpub.com/sites/default/files/downloads/Swift 2 Design patterns_ColorImages.pdf.

# Errata

Although we have taken every care to ensure the accuracy of our content, mistakes do happen. If you find a mistake in one of our books—maybe a mistake in the text or the code—we would be grateful if you could report this to us. By doing so, you can save other readers from frustration and help us improve subsequent versions of this book. If you find any errata, please report them by visiting http://www.packtpub.com/submit-errata, selecting your book, clicking on the **Errata Submission Form** link, and entering the details of your errata. Once your errata are verified, your submission will be accepted and the errata will be uploaded to our website or added to any list of existing errata under the Errata section of that title.

To view the previously submitted errata, go to https://www.packtpub.com/books/content/support and enter the name of the book in the search field. The required information will appear under the **Errata** section.

# Piracy

Piracy of copyrighted material on the Internet is an ongoing problem across all media. At Packt, we take the protection of our copyright and licenses very seriously. If you come across any illegal copies of our works in any form on the Internet, please provide us with the location address or website name immediately so that we can pursue a remedy.

Please contact us at copyright@packtpub.com with a link to the suspected pirated material.

We appreciate your help in protecting our authors and our ability to bring you valuable content.

# eBooks, discount offers, and more

Did you know that Packt offers eBook versions of every book published, with PDF and ePub files available? You can upgrade to the eBook version at www.PacktPub.com and as a print book customer, you are entitled to a discount on the eBook copy. Get in touch with us at customercare@packtpub.com for more details.

At www.PacktPub.com, you can also read a collection of free technical articles, sign up for a range of free newsletters, and receive exclusive discounts and offers on Packt books and eBooks.

# Questions

If you have a problem with any aspect of this book, you can contact us at questions@packtpub.com, and we will do our best to address the problem.

# 1
# Creational Patterns

The creational patterns are designed to deal with the object creation mechanism in software designing. A system using these patterns becomes independent of how objects are created, which means it is independent of how concrete classes are instantiated.

These patterns encapsulate the use of concrete classes and favor the use of interfaces in the relationship between objects, allowing to have better abstraction of the global system conception.

Thus, if we analyze the **singleton** pattern, a pattern designed to instantiate only one instance of a class, we find that the mechanism that controls the unique access to this instance is fully encapsulated in the class, which means that this is completely transparent to the client consuming the instance of the class.

In this chapter, we will introduce you to the five creational patterns and discuss how we can use them with Swift:

- The prototype pattern
- The factory method pattern
- The singleton pattern
- The abstract factory pattern
- The builder pattern

The objectives of these patterns are described in the following table:

| Pattern | Objective |
|---|---|
| The prototype pattern | This pattern allows you to create new objects by duplicating existing objects called prototypes. This pattern has the cloning capability. |
| The factory method pattern | This pattern introduces you to an abstract method that allows you to create an object by telling its subclasses about the effective creation of the object. |
| The singleton pattern | This pattern ensures that a class has only one instance. This class provides a unique point of access that returns this instance. |
| The abstract factory pattern | This pattern allows you to create an object that is grouped in families by hiding the concrete classes that are needed to create these objects. |
| The builder pattern | This pattern allows you to separate the creation of complex objects from their implementation. This permits a client to create complex objects having different representations. |

# The prototype pattern

Our first pattern will be the prototype pattern; we will see how we can use it to accelerate the creation of an instance. We will see how we can use it to copy an existing instance, and eventually, we will see how to modify the new one to our needs.

# Roles

The prototype pattern is used to create a new object by duplicating existing objects called **prototypes**, and they have a cloning capability.

This pattern is used in the following use cases:

- When you need to create an instance without knowing the hierarchy of a class
- When you need to create class instances that are dynamically loaded
- When you need to have a simple object system and not include a parallel hierarchy of a factory class

# Design

The following diagram shows the generic class of the prototype pattern:

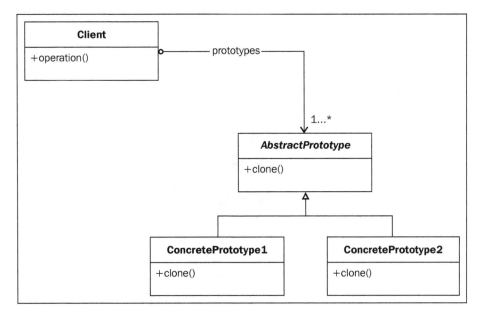

# Participants

Participant to this pattern are as follows:

- Client: This class contains a list of objects called prototypes that are instances of the AbstractPrototype abstract class. The Client class needs to clone these prototypes without having to know their internal structure and subclass hierarchy.
- AbstractPrototype: This is an abstract class that can duplicate itself. This class contains a cloning method called clone().
- ConcretePrototype1 and ConcretePrototype2: These are concrete classes that inherit from the AbstractPrototype class. They define a prototype and have both a cloning method called clone().

# Collaborations

The client asks to one or more prototypes to clone themselves.

# Illustration

A simple and real example of where this pattern can be applied is the famous game *HeartStone* from *Blizzard* (the creator of *World of Warcraft*). In this strategy card game, when you spend "mana" to use spells, weapons, or put a minion on the board, there is a special minion that has the ability to clone a particular card. When a player uses this card, it selects the minion that he or she wants to clone and the card becomes an exact copy of the selected card. The following card represent the "HeartStone" card that have this behavior:

# Implementation

The following code represent the implementation of the pattern using Swift:

```swift
import UIKit

class AbstractCard {
  var name: String?
  var mana: Int?
  var attack: Int?
  var defense: Int?

  init(name:String?, mana:Int?, attack:Int?, defense:Int?) {
    self.name = name
```

```
        self.attack = attack
        self.defense = defense
        self.mana = mana
    }

    func clone() -> AbstractCard {
      return AbstractCard(name: self.name, mana: self.mana, attack:
      self.attack, defense: self.defense)
    }
}

class Card: AbstractCard {

    override init(name:String?, mana:Int?, attack:Int?, defense:Int?
    ) {
      super.init(name: name,mana: mana,attack: attack,defense:
      defense)

    }
}
```

 The Abstract Prototype class is our AbstractCard class, where we implement a way to return a copy of itself using the clone() method.

# Usage

The following code simulate how the client will interact with the Card object which implement the prototype pattern:

```
// Simulate our client

// This is the card that we will copy
let raidLeader = Card(name: "Raid Leader", mana: 3, attack: 2,
  defense: 2)

// Now we use our faceless Manipulator card to clone the
  raidleader
let facelessManipulator = raidLeader.clone()

print("\(facelessManipulator.name, facelessManipulator.mana,
  facelessManipulator.attack, facelessManipulator.defense)")
```

Since the code is written in a Playground file, you should consider it as the code that you'll put in the `Client` class.

First, we instantiate a new card named `Raid Leader`. This is a concrete prototype class. Let say that you have the "Faceless Manipulator" card and you want to use it to clone the "Raid Leader" card, then you simply need to use the `raidLeader.clone()` method that will return a new instance with the exact same properties as "Raid Leader".

By checking the details on the right-hand side of the Playground file, you'll see that the `facelessManipulator` constant has exactly the same properties as `raidLeader` (line 39), as shown in the following screenshot:

```
36  // now we use our faceless Manipulator card
       to clone the raidleader
37  let facelessManipulator = raidLeader.clone()     AbstractCard
38
39  print("\(facelessManipulator.name,                "(Optional("Raid Leader"), Optional(3), Optional(2), Optional(2))\n"
       facelessManipulator.mana,
       facelessManipulator.attack,
       facelessManipulator.defense)")


       (Optional("Raid Leader"), Optional(3),
              Optional(2), Optional(2))
```

# The factory method pattern

Our second pattern is a very well-known pattern. It introduces you to the famous concept: "Program to an interface, not an implementation." The instantiation is done in the factory class that depends on the type that we need and the type that needs to be returned to the client.

## Roles

The factory method pattern is one of the most used patterns in software designs. The purpose of this pattern is to abstract the creation of an object. The factory method lets a class defer instantiation to subclasses.

You'll see from that time to time that we have mentioned "program to an interface." This is exactly what this pattern does. With Swift, instead of an interface, you'll code with the "protocol" instead of the class itself.

This pattern is used in the following use cases:

- A class only knows about abstract classes or interfaces of objects with whom it has some relationships
- A class wants its subclasses to instantiate the object in order to benefit of polymorphism mechanism

# Design

The following diagram shows the generic class of the factory method pattern:

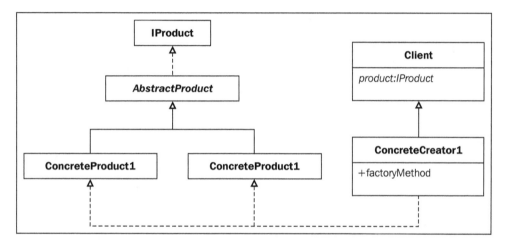

# Participants

Participant to this pattern are as follows:

- **Product interface**: This class contains the definition of our product. We will define what a card is here.
- **Abstract product**: This abstract class implements the signature of our cards and some methods. You'll see that we keep the prototype pattern that allows us to eventually clone a card. These classes define the properties of our products.
- **Concrete product**: This class defines our product; in our example, the `Raid Leader` card is a concrete product, such as the `Faceless Manipulator` card.
- **Concrete creator**: This class implements our factory method.

# Illustration

In our previous pattern, you would have seen the following line:

```
let raidLeader = Card(name: "Raid Leader", mana: 3, attack: 2,
  defense: 2)
```

Here, we directly program an implementation. We need a way to create some cards, but without having the knowledge to know exactly how to construct the card; we can only tell to create the `raidLeader` and `Faceless Manipulator` cards. At this point of time, the client doesn't want to know that the `Raid Leader` card needs three manas, so it provides two points of attack and two points of defense.

# Implementation

The implementation of the factory method pattern is as follows:

```
import UIKit
import Foundation

//Define what a card is
protocol Card {
  var name: String? {get set}
  var attack: Int? {get set}
  var defense: Int? {get set}
  var mana: Int? {get set}
  func clone() -> Card
  func toString() -> String
}

// AbstractCard
// implements the signature and some properties
class AbstractCard: NSObject, Card {
  private var _name: String?
  private var _mana: Int?
  private var _attack: Int?
  private var _defense: Int?

  init(name: String?, mana: Int?, attack: Int?, defense: Int?) {
    self._name = name
    self._attack = attack
    self._defense = defense
    self._mana = mana
    super.init()
  }
```

```
  override init(){
    super.init()
  }

  //property name
  var name: String?{
    get{ return _name }
    set{ _name = newValue }
  }

  //property mana
  var mana: Int? {
    get{ return _mana }
    set{ _mana = newValue }
  }

  //property attack
  var attack: Int? {
    get{ return _attack }
    set{ _attack = newValue }
  }

  //property attack
  var defense: Int? {
    get{ return _defense }
    set{ _defense = newValue }
  }

  func clone() -> Card {
    return AbstractCard(name: self.name, mana: self.mana, attack:
    self.attack, defense: self.defense)
  }

  func toString() -> String{
    return ("\(self.name, self.mana, self.attack,self.defense)")
  }
}

enum CardType {
  case FacelessManipulator, RaidLeader
}
```

```
// our Factory Class
// Depending what we need, this class return an instance of the
// appropriate object.
class CardFactory{
  class func createCard(cardtype: CardType) -> Card?{

    switch cardtype {
    case .FacelessManipulator:
      return FacelessManipulatorCard()
    case .RaidLeader:
      return RaidLeaderCard()
    default:
      return nil
    }
  }
}


//Concrete Card "Raid Leader"
//This is the full definition of the Raid Leader Card
class RaidLeaderCard: AbstractCard {
  override init()
  {
    super.init()
    self._mana = 3
    self._attack = 2
    self._defense = 2
    self._name = "Raid Leader"
  }
}


//Concrete Card "Faceless Manipulator"
//this is the full definition of the FacelessManipulator Card.
class FacelessManipulatorCard: AbstractCard {
  override init()
  {
    super.init()
    self._mana = 5
    self._attack = 3
    self._defense = 3
    self._name = "Faceless Manipulator"


  }
}
```

# Usage

To simulate the use of the factory method pattern by a client, we can write the card creation as follows:

```
//simulate our client

var c = CardFactory.createCard(.FacelessManipulator)
c?.toString()
```

To simulate our client, we simply tell the CardFactory method that we want a FacelessManipulator card.

To do this, we use the createCard method (our factory method), and this method will delegate the instantiation of the card that was asked.

The variable c has the type Card and not FacelessManipulator.

# The singleton pattern

This pattern is certainly the pattern that every developer learns first. It is often used with a factory or abstract factory class to ensure that there is only one instance of the class.

# Roles

The singleton pattern ensures that a class has only one instance and provides a global point of access to it, and at this point, it returns an instance of this class.

In some cases, it can be useful to have some classes that have only one instance; for example, in the case of the abstract factory, where it is not useful to have several instances.

# Design

The following figure shows the generic UML class diagram of the singleton pattern. There are many way to write the singleton pattern using Swift.

Here, we use the easiest way to do this. With Swift, you'll see that we can change the way in which we apply it, thanks to the class constant:

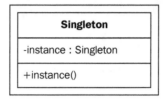

# Participants

There is only one participant in this pattern: the `Singleton` class.

This class provides a method that returns only one instance of the class. The mechanism locks the creation of other instances. It was introduced with Swift 1.2. We can now use class constants.

With Swift 1.2, we will use the class constants to provide us with a way to ensure the unique creation of the instance.

A class constant is defined as follows:

```
static let myVariable = myObject()
```

# Collaborations

Every client will have access to the unique instance of the `Singleton` class by calling the `Instance` method.

With Swift, the approach we'll consider is the one that accesses our unique instance of the `Singleton` class using the class constant that we will call `sharedInstance`.

# Illustration

You are developing your card game and you need to manage all the data of the current game. In our game, we have two players; each player has a deck, mana reserve, name, and so on. We have a board (the table where we put our cards) and a game state (who is currently playing). To manage all of this information, you'll need a `BoardManager` class. This class will be a singleton class because we will not have several boards at the same time (we only allow one game at a time). The singleton pattern can be something interesting that can be used here in order to make sure that we access the good data.

# Implementation

The following approach supports lazy initialization, and it is thread safe by the definition of `let`:

```
import UIKit

class BoardGameManager {

  static let sharedInstance = BoardGameManager()
  init() {
    println("Singleton initialized");
  }

}
```

# Usage

To use our singleton object, each client will access it using the following code :

```
let boardManager = BoardGameManager.sharedInstance
```

The `boardManager` variable contains all the members available in our singleton object and will be initialized only once.

This pattern is used in the following cases:

*   We must have only one instance of a class
*   This instance must be accessible to clients from a well-known access point

# The abstract factory pattern

We already introduced you to a very popular concept in design patterns: **factories**. Factories are the classes that handle the instantiation of related objects without subclassing. The factory method pattern that we have already seen hides the class name from where an object is instantiated. The abstract factory pattern is more complete as it creates families of related or dependent objects.

# Roles

The abstract factory pattern is designed to build objects grouped in families without having to know the concrete class needed to create the object.

This pattern is generally used in the following domains:

- A system that uses products needs to stay independent of how these products are grouped and instantiated
- A system can have several product families that can evolve

# Design

The following diagram represents the generic structure of the abstract factory pattern. You will see how products and families are decoupled:

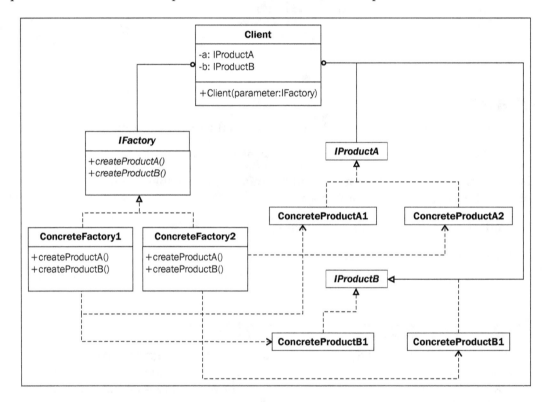

# Participants

The abstract factory pattern has a lot of participants:

- Abstract Factory: This abstract class defines the signature of the different methods that create our products.

- ConcreteFactory1 and ConcreteFactory2: These are our concrete classes that implement our methods for each products' families. By knowing the family and product, the factory is able to create an instance of the product for that family.

- IProductA and IProductB: These are our interfaces that define our products that are independent of their family. A family is introduced in their concrete subclasses.

- ProductA and ProductB: These are the concrete classes that implement IProductA and IProductB, respectively.

# Collaborations

The Client class uses one instance of one of the concrete factories to create products throughout the interface of the abstract factory.

# Illustration

Our company specializes in manufacturing watches. Our watches are built in two parts: a band and dial. Our watches come in two sizes, so we must adapt the manufacturing of the band and dial according to the size of our watch.

In order to simplify how to manage the manufacturing of our watches, the direction team decided to use one manufacturer who specializes in products that are adapted to the 38 mm model of our watch, and another manufacturer whose products are adapted to the 42 mm model of our watch.

Each of these manufacturers will build a dial and band that are adapted to the dimension of the watch.

# Implementation

To implement our pattern, we first need to identify our actors. The two manufacturers represent the ConcreteFactory1 and ConcreteFactory2 classes. These two factories implement the AbstractFactory method, which tell us that we can create a band or dial. Of course, the concrete factories will create the dial adapted to the size of the watch produced in that manufacture.

Our ConcreteProductA and ConcreteProductB classes are the band and the dial; each of these products implements their respective IProductA and IProductB interfaces, as shown in the following code:

```
import UIKit

//Our interfaces
protocol IWatchBand {
  var color: UIColor{get set}
  var size: BandSize{get set}
  var type: BandType{get set}
  init(size: BandSize)
}

protocol IWatchDial {
  var material: MaterialType{get set}
  var size: WatchSize{get set}
  init(size: WatchSize)
}

//Enums
enum MaterialType: String {
  case Aluminium = "Aluminium",
  StainlessSteel = "Stainless Steel",
  Gold = "Gold"
}

enum BandType: String {
  case Milanese = "Milanese",
  Classic = "Classic",
  Leather = "Leather",
  Modern = "Modern",
  LinkBracelet = "LinkBracelet",
  SportBand = "SportBand"
}
```

```
enum WatchSize: String {
  case _38mm = "38mm", _42mm = "42mm"
}

enum BandSize: String {
  case SM = "SM", ML = "ML"
}

//prepare our Bands components
class MilaneseBand: IWatchBand {
  var color = UIColor.yellowColor()
  var size: BandSize
  var type = BandType.Milanese
  required init(size _size: BandSize) {
    size = _size
  }
 }

class Classic: IWatchBand {
  var color = UIColor.yellowColor()
  var size: BandSize
  var type = BandType.Classic
  required init(size _size: BandSize) {
    size = _size
  }
}
class Leather:IWatchBand{
  var color = UIColor.yellowColor()
  var size:BandSize
  var type = BandType.Leather
  required init(size _size: BandSize) {
    size = _size
  }
}
class Modern: IWatchBand {
  var color = UIColor.yellowColor()
  var size: BandSize
  var type = BandType.Modern
  required init(size _size: BandSize) {
    size = _size
  }
}
```

```
class LinkBracelet: IWatchBand {
  var color = UIColor.yellowColor()
  var size: BandSize
  var type = BandType.LinkBracelet
  required init(size _size: BandSize) {
    size = _size
  }
}
class SportBand: IWatchBand {
  var color = UIColor.yellowColor()
  var size: BandSize
  var type = BandType.SportBand
  required init(size _size: BandSize) {
    size = _size
  }
}


//Dials
class AluminiumDial: IWatchDial {
  var material: MaterialType = MaterialType.Aluminium
  var size: WatchSize
  required init(size _size:WatchSize){
    size = _size
  }
}

class StainlessSteelDial: IWatchDial {
  var material: MaterialType = MaterialType.StainlessSteel
  var size: WatchSize
  required init(size _size:WatchSize){
    size = _size
  }
}

class GoldDial: IWatchDial {
  var material: MaterialType = MaterialType.Gold
  var size: WatchSize
  required init(size _size:WatchSize){
    size = _size
  }
}
```

```swift
//Our AbstractFactory
class WatchFactory {

  func createBand(bandType: BandType) -> IWatchBand {
    fatalError("not implemented")
  }
  func createDial(materialtype: MaterialType) -> IWatchDial{
    fatalError("not implemented")
  }

  //our static method that return the appropriated factory.
  final class func getFactory(size: WatchSize) -> WatchFactory{
    var factory: WatchFactory?
    switch(size){
    case ._38mm:
      factory = Watch38mmFactory()
    case ._42mm:
      factory = Watch42mmFactory()
    }
    return factory!
  }

}


// Concrete Factory 1 for 42 mm
class Watch42mmFactory: WatchFactory {
  override func createBand(bandType: BandType) -> IWatchBand {
    switch bandType {
    case .Milanese:
      return MilaneseBand(size: .ML)
    case .Classic:
      return Classic(size: .ML)
    case .Leather:
      return Leather(size: .ML)
    case .LinkBracelet:
      return LinkBracelet(size: .ML)
    case .Modern:
      return Modern(size: .ML)
    case .SportBand:
      return SportBand(size: .ML)
    default:
      return SportBand(size: .ML)
    }
```

```
    }

    override func createDial(materialtype: MaterialType) ->
    IWatchDial {
      switch materialtype{
      case MaterialType.Gold:
        return GoldDial(size: ._42mm)
      case MaterialType.StainlessSteel:
        return StainlessSteelDial(size: ._42mm)
      case MaterialType.Aluminium:
        return AluminiumDial(size: ._42mm)
      }
    }
}

//Concrete Factory 2 for 38mm
class Watch38mmFactory: WatchFactory{
  override func createBand(bandType:BandType) -> IWatchBand {
    switch bandType {
    case .Milanese:
      return MilaneseBand(size: .SM)
    case .Classic:
      return Classic(size: .SM)
    case .Leather:
      return Leather(size: .SM)
    case .LinkBracelet:
      return LinkBracelet(size: .SM)
    case .Modern:
      return Modern(size: .SM)
    case .SportBand:
      return SportBand(size: .SM)
    default:
      return SportBand(size: .SM)
    }
  }

  override func createDial(materialtype: MaterialType) ->
  IWatchDial {
    switch materialtype{
    case MaterialType.Gold:
      return GoldDial(size: ._38mm)
    case MaterialType.Gold:
      return StainlessSteelDial(size: ._38mm)
    case MaterialType.Gold:
```

```
    return AluminiumDial(size: ._38mm)
  default:
    return AluminiumDial(size: ._38mm)


  }
 }
}
```

# Usage

To simulate our client, we will use the following code:

```
//Here we deliver products from the Manufacture 1 specialized in
//products for the 38 mm Watch
let manufacture1 = WatchFactory.getFactory(WatchSize._38mm)
let productA = manufacture1.createBand(BandType.Milanese)
productA.color
productA.size.rawValue
productA.type.rawValue

let productB = manufacture1.createDial(MaterialType.Gold)
productB.material.rawValue
productB.size.rawValue


//Here we delivers products from the Manufacture 2 specialized in
//products for the 42 mm Watch
let manufacture2 = WatchFactory.getFactory(WatchSize._42mm)
let productC = manufacture2.createBand(BandType.LinkBracelet)
productC.color
productC.size.rawValue
productC.type.rawValue

let productD = manufacture2.createDial(MaterialType.Gold)
productD.material.rawValue
productD.size.rawValue
```

The Playground file will display our product's properties, depending on the factory used. The details of product *A* (the band) and product *B* (the dial) from the `manufacture1` object are shown in the following screenshot:

```
Watch38mmFactory
MilaneseBand
    r 1,0 g 1,0 b 0,0 a 1,0
"SM"
"Milanese"

GoldDial
"Gold"
"38mm"
```

The details of product *C* (the band) and product *D* (the dial) from the `manufacture2` object are shown in the following screenshot:

```
Watch42mmFactory
LinkBracelet
    r 1,0 g 1,0 b 0,0 a 1,0
"ML"
"LinkBracelet"

GoldDial
"Gold"
"42mm"
```

The sizes of the band and the dial adapt to the manufacturer who delivers the product.

 We should use the singleton pattern to ensure that we have only one instance of our abstract factory. This instance can be shared between several clients.

# The builder pattern

Unlike the abstract factory pattern, which will produce parts of products of the same family, the builder pattern will help us build the finalized product that consists of several parts.

# Roles

The main purpose of the builder pattern is to abstract the building of complex objects from its actual construction. Having the same construction process can create different representations of the product.

This pattern can be used when:

- A client needs to construct complex objects without having to know its implementation
- A client needs to construct complex objects that need to have several implementations or representations

# Design

The following figure shows the generic UML class diagram of the builder pattern:

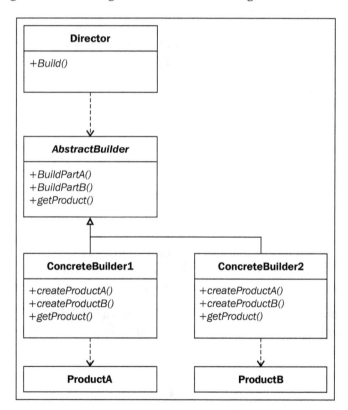

# Participants

This pattern is quite simple as it has only a few participants:

- `Director`: This class constructs the product using the interface of the `AbstractBuilder` class.

- `AbstractBuilder`: This class defines the method signature that allows the construction of all the parts of the product, and it contains a signature of a method that returns the product once this is built.

- `ConcreteBuilder`: This is the `Concrete` class that implements the method of the `AbstractBuilder` class.

- `Product`: This is the finalized product. The product contains all the parts of the watch.

# Collaborations

The client creates the `ConcreteBuilder` and `Director` classes. The `Director` class will then build an object if the client asks him to do so by invoking the constructor and returns the finalized product to the client.

# Illustration

Using the `AbstractFactory` method, we can use the builder pattern to build a watch. As we've seen that a watch has several parts: a dial and band. A watch can have two sizes too, and as we have already seen, the representation of the dial or band depends on the size of the watch too.

# Implementation

If we want to build some watches that are represented with a dial and band, we will define a `Director` class that will define the construction order of all the parts of our watches and return the finalized watch to the client.

The `Director` class will call all the constructors who are in charge to construct one part of the watch. To implement this, we will reuse the existing code of the abstract factory pattern and add the following code.

Open the `Builder.playground` file in Xcode to see the added code at the bottom of the file:

```
//Our builder1
class BuilderGoldMilanese38mmWatch: AbstractWatchBuilder {
  override func buildDial() {
    watch.band = MilaneseBand(size: BandSize.SM)
  }
  override func buildBand() {
    watch.dial = GoldDial(size: WatchSize._38mm)
  }
}

//Our builder2
class BuilderAluminiumSportand42mmWatch:AbstractWatchBuilder {
  override func buildDial() {
    watch.band = SportBand(size: BandSize.ML)
  }
  override func buildBand() {
    watch.dial = AluminiumDial(size: WatchSize._42mm)
  }
}

//our Director class
class Director {
  var builder: AbstractWatchBuilder?
  init(){

  }

  func buildWatch(builder: AbstractWatchBuilder){
    builder.buildBand()
    builder.buildDial()
  }
}
```

# Usage

To simulate our client, we will tell our director to create two watches:

- A 42 mm aluminium dial with a sports band
- A 38 mm gold dial with a milanese band

The code for the example is as follows:

```
//We will build 2 Watches :
//First is the Aluminium Dial of 42mm with Sport Band
let director = Director()
var b1 = BuilderAluminiumSportand42mmWatch()
director.buildWatch(b1)

// our watch 1
var w1 = b1.getResult()
w1.band?.color
w1.band?.type.rawValue
w1.band?.size.rawValue
w1.dial?.size.rawValue
w1.dial?.material.rawValue

//Our 2nd watch is a Gold 38mm Dial with Milanese Band
var b2 = BuilderGoldMilanese38mmWatch ()
director.buildWatch(b2)

// Our watch 1
var w2 = b2.getResult()
w2.band?.color
w2.band?.type.rawValue
w2.band?.size.rawValue
w2.dial?.size.rawValue
w2.dial?.material.rawValue
```

The result is shown in Playground like this:

```
Watch
    r 1,0 g 1,0 b 0,0 a 1,0
"SportBand"
"ML"
"42mm"
"Aluminium"


BuilderGoldMilanese38mmWatch
Director


Watch
    r 1,0 g 1,0 b 0,0 a 1,0
"Milanese"
"SM"
"38mm"
"Gold"
```

Swift allows the use of closure that simplifies the creation of our complex objects. Regarding the example that we provided earlier, we can write the following code to build our two watches.

# Implementation using closures

Here, we don't need to use the `Director` and `ConcreteBuilder` classes. Instead, we will tell our `Watch` class that the builder will be in the closure.

In the previous example, remove the `Director`, `AbstractBuilder`, and `ConcreteBuilder` classes.

We just need to write the `Watch` class, as shown in the following code (you can find the following code in the `BuilderClosures.playground` file accompanying this chapter):

```
//our Product Class : a Watch
//The builder will be in the closure
class Watch{
  var dial:IWatchDial?
  var band:IWatchBand?
  typealias buildWatchClosure = (Watch) -> Void

  init(build:buildWatchClosure){
    build(self)
  }
}
```

Then, to simulate our client, we can write the following code which will call the appropriate constructor assigned to the band or dial property of the `Watch` object:

```
//Simulate our clients

let Gold42mmMilaneseWatch = Watch(build: {
  $0.band = MilaneseBand(size: BandSize.ML)
  $0.dial = GoldDial(size: WatchSize._42mm)
})
```

The result is as follows:

```
   r 1,0 g 1,0 b 0,0 a 1,0
"Milanese"
"ML"
"Gold"
"42mm"


Watch
Watch
Watch


   r 1,0 g 1,0 b 0,0 a 1,0
"SportBand"
"SM"
"Aluminium"
"38mm"
```

# Summary

Well, I hope that this chapter was a good introduction to the use of patterns using Swift. We learned the five creational patterns: the prototype pattern, the factory method pattern, the singleton pattern, the abstract factory pattern, and the builder pattern. We also learned when to use them and how to implement them.

In the next chapter, we will introduce you to three structural patterns that are designed to ease the relationship between entities.

# 2
# Structural Patterns – Decorator, Proxy, and Bridge

After reviewing the five creational patterns in the previous chapter, we will now talk about another category of patterns: the structural patterns. There are seven patterns to talk about; these patterns ease the design by identifying a simple way to realize relationships between entities.

We will see how these patterns help you to encapsulate the composition of objects through the use of an interface, allowing you to conveniently abstract your system as the creational pattern does to encapsulate the creation of objects. Structural patterns highlight the use of interfaces.

You will see how the composition is designed; we will not interfere with the object itself but with the one that will transfer the structuration. This second object is strongly related to the first one. Indeed, the first object presents the interface to the client and manages its relationship with the second object, which, manages the composition and doesn't have any interfaces with clients.

One important thing to make a note of is that this structuration allows a great flexibility to your system by allowing dynamic modification of the composition. Indeed, we can substitute an object with another if both inherit the same class and use the same interface.

# Static and dynamic composition

We can have several possible implementations. The classic way to design this is to differentiate these implementations in subclasses. In this case, we will provide an interface from where our classes will implement this interface.

This solution consists of a static composition. Indeed, once the implementation class of an object is chosen, we can no longer change it. The following diagram is the implementation of an object by heritage:

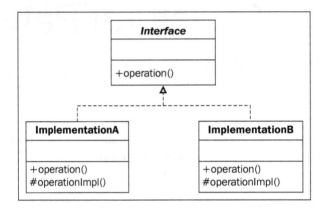

Another way is to separate the implementation in another object. The implementation parts are managed by an instance of the ConcreteImplementationA class or by the ConcreteImplementationB class. This reference is referred by the implementation attribute. This instance can then be easily substituted by another instance at runtime. This composition is dynamic.

The following UML class diagram shows us clearly how to structure your objects using a dynamic composition. The ConcreteImplementation class can be switched at runtime, without having to modify the Realization object.

We can eventually modify the realization object, without having to modify our original object, as shown in the following diagram:

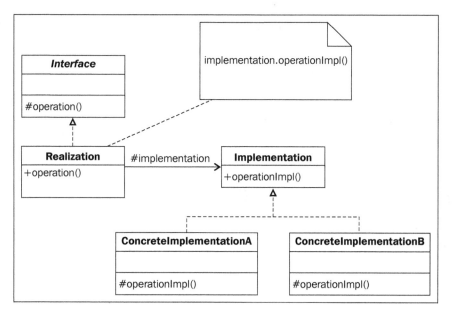

In this chapter, you'll see how to use this solution with the bridge pattern.

The discovery of the structural patterns will span three chapters. In this chapter, we will introduce you to three of them:

- The decorator pattern
- The proxy pattern
- The bridge pattern

These three patterns provide a mechanism of adding states and behaviors dynamically, controlling the creation and access of objects, and keeping the specification and implementation separate.

The objectives of the three structural patterns that we will see in this chapter are described in the following table:

| Pattern | Objective |
| --- | --- |
| The decorator pattern | This pattern allows you to dynamically add new behaviors and functionalities to the object. |
| The proxy pattern | This pattern is a substitute of another object. It provides a behavior that can adapt to the optimization or security needs. |
| The bridge pattern | This pattern decouples an abstraction from its implementation, enabling them to vary independently. |

# The decorator pattern

The first structural pattern that we will discuss is the decorator pattern. It introduces you to the object substitution by adding new functionalities or behaviors.

## Roles

The main objective of this pattern is to dynamically add new functionalities to an object. The interface of the object will not be modified, so from the client's perspective, this is fully transparent.

This pattern is an alternative to the addition of a subclass that adds functionalities to its parent class. A key implementation point in the decorator pattern is that decorators both inherit the original class and contain an instantiation of it.

This pattern can be used when:

- A system adds dynamically new functionalities to an object, without having to modify its interface, which means without having to modify the client of this object
- A system manages the behavior that can be dynamically removed
- The use of inheritance is not a good option because of an already complex class hierarchy

# Design

The generic UML class diagram of the decorator pattern is quiet simple: The ConcreteComponent and AbstractDecorator classes share the same interface that have the same method name. Our AbstractDecorator class defines a constructor where we pass our Abstractcomponent class as an argument. Then, in our ConcreteDecorator class, we reroute the operation call to the additionalOperation methods to add new functionalities or behaviors to the original component, as shown in the following diagram:

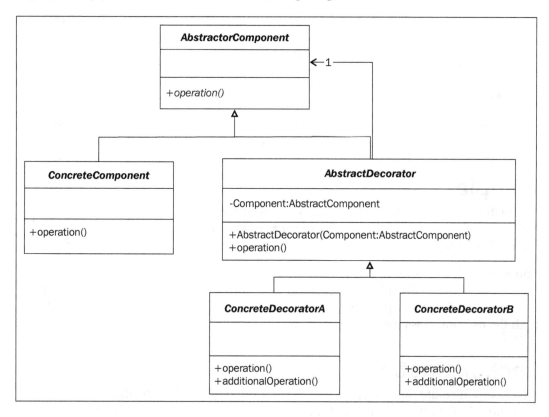

# Participants

In the preceding diagram, there are four participants in this pattern:

- AbstractComponent: This is the common interface to components and decorators.
- ConcreteComponent: This is the main object to which we want to add behaviors and/or functionalities.
- AbstractDecorator: This abstract class contains a reference to a component.
- ConcreteDecoratorA and ConcreteDecoratorB: These are the concrete subclasses of AbstractDecorator. These classes implement the functionalities added to the component.

# Collaboration

When a decorator receives a message that must reach the component, it redirects the message by making a prior or posterior operation to that redirection.

# Sample

To illustrate this pattern, we will take a simple example. Let's suppose that you have a drawing software that enables you to draw some shapes on the screen: a rectangle and square.

You already know how to draw these shapes. Now, you need to add a new functionality that will add a rounded angle to your shapes. To do this, you need to decide which decorator pattern you need to use that will allow you to not to interfere with the existing class method signature.

# Implementation

First, we will create our interface that defines the shape. We will simulate a Draw() operation. In fact, the method will return a string that tells us what is drawn:

```
protocol IShape {
   func draw() -> String
}
```

Now, we will create our two concrete classes that implement the IShape interface. We will have the Square and Rectangle classes. They both implement the draw function. This function returns the shape that is currently drawn:

```
class Square: IShape {
  func draw() -> String{
    return "drawing Shape: Square"
  }
}

class Rectangle: IShape {
  func draw() -> String {
    return "drawing Shape: Rectangle"
  }
}
```

Our classes are ready; now, we prepare our abstract ShapeDecorator class that defines the structure of our future concrete decorators. This class implements the IShape interface too, so the Draw() function must be present. Nevertheless, Swift doesn't have an abstract class, so we implement the draw method, but we force an exception to tell us that this method must be implemented. The ShapeDecorator class will not be used by the client itself. The client will call the ConcreteDecorator object to add a new functionality to its shape:

```
class ShapeDecorator: IShape {
  private let decoratedShape: IShape

  required init(decoratedShape: IShape){
    self.decoratedShape = decoratedShape
  }

   func draw() -> String {
     fatalError("Not Implemented")
  }
}
```

Now, we add our concrete decorator class that inherits from the ShapeDecorator abstract class. We add our new setRoundedCornerShape functionality to this class and override the draw function to return the shape that is drawn, but with rounded corners:

```
class RoundedCornerShapeDecorator: ShapeDecorator{
  required init(decoratedShape: IShape) {
```

```
        super.init(decoratedShape: decoratedShape)
    }

    override func draw() ->String{
      //we concatenate our shape properties
      return  decoratedShape.draw() + "," +
      setRoundedCornerShape(decoratedShape)
    }

    func setRoundedCornerShape(decoratedShape: IShape) -> String{
      return "Corners are rounded"
    }
}
```

# Usage

Now, here is the easy part that shows us how to use all of the code, we already have written, from the client perspective.

We first create our two concrete shapes:

```
let rectangle = Rectangle()
let square = Square()
```

Now, we want to have some shapes with rounded corners. To do this, we simply call the ConcreteDecorator class that interests us, the RoundedCornerShapeDecorator class, and pass a new shape (Rectangle or Square) as an argument of the constructor:

```
let roundedRectangle = RoundedCornerShapeDecorator(decoratedShape:
    Rectangle())

let roundedSquare = RoundedCornerShapeDecorator(decoratedShape:
    Square())
```

Now, we simulate the Draw() method on the screen of our shapes by calling the draw operation:

```
print("rectangle with Normal Angles")
rectangle.draw()

print("square with Normal Angles")
square.draw()

//rounded corners shapes
roundedRectangle.draw()
roundedSquare.draw()
```

The Playground will return the following result:

```
"rectangle with Normal Angles\n"
"drawing Shape: Rectangle"

"square with Normal Angles\n"
"drawing Shape: Square"


"Rounded border rectangle\n"
"drawing Shape: Rectangle,Corners are rounded"


"drawing Shape: Square,Corners are rounded"
```

Swift allows you to implement the decorator pattern using the concept of extensions. This allows you to add additional methods to concrete classes or constructs, without having to subclass or alter the original one. With extensions, you can add new methods but no new properties, as opposed to a subclass.

# The proxy pattern

The second pattern that we will talk about in this chapter is the proxy pattern. It is often used for security or optimization purposes.

## Roles

The objective of the proxy pattern is to substitute an object (the subject) with another one that will control its access. The object that substitutes the subject shares the same interface, so it is transparent from the consumer's perspective. The proxy is often a small (public) object that stands in for a more complex (private) object that is activated once certain circumstances are clear. The proxy adds a level of indirection by accepting requests from a client object and passing them to the real subject as necessary.

The proxy pattern is used in object-oriented programming. There are several types of proxies, which are as follows:

- **A virtual proxy**: This allows you to create a "big" object at the appropriate time (used when the creation process is slow)

- **A remote proxy**: This allows you to access an object that is available on another environment (such as on a multiplayer game server)

- **An authentication proxy**: This check whether the access permission for a request is correct or not

# Design

The following class diagram is quite simple; we have an interface that defines our subject, both the proxy and RealSubject implement this interface.

The client will call the proxy, not the RealSubject object himself. The proxy contains a reference to the RealSubject object. When the proxy receives a request, it can analyze it, and if the request is considered to be valid, it can be rerouted to the RealSubject.request() method. The proxy can decide when to create, or not, the RealSubject object avoiding to have to manage too big object in memory if useless. The following figure represent the generic class diagram of the proxy pattern:

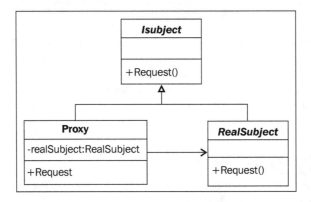

# Participants

There are only three participants in this pattern:

- ISubject: This is the common interface of the Proxy and RealSubject object

- RealSubject: This is the object that is controlled and manipulated by the proxy.

- Proxy: This is the object that substitutes RealSubject. It has the same interface of the RealSubject object (the ISubject interface). It creates, controls, enhances, and authenticates access to a RealSubject object.

# Collaboration

The proxy receives the incoming request from a client instead of the RealSubject. If necessary, the message is then delegated to the RealSubject object. In this case, prior to the delegation, the proxy creates the RealSubject object if it has not already been done.

# Illustration

We are developing a new software; this software presents a video catalog in a list. For each video in the list, we have a placeholder for the video and a description. The placeholder of the video first displays a screenshot of the video. If we click on this image, the video will be launched.

The video catalog contains videos, so it will be too heavy to have all of these videos in memory and transferring them through the network will take too long. The proxy pattern will help us organize all of this. We will create the subject only when we will need it, once the screenshot is clicked.

The two advantages are as follows:

- The list is loaded quickly, mainly if it is downloaded from the network
- Only videos that we want to watch are created, loaded, and played

The `Screenshot` class that represents the video is called the proxy of the `Video` subject. The proxy substitutes the `Video` subject for the display. The `Screenshot` class implements the same interface as the `Video` subject (the `RealSubject` object).

In our example, the proxy pattern design is as follows:

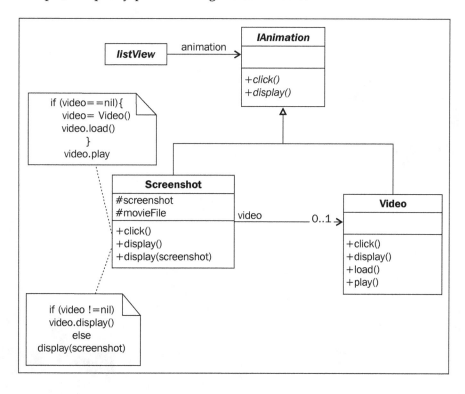

When the proxy receives the `display()` message, it will display the video if this one already exists. If it receives the `click()` message, it will first create the `Video` subject and then load the video.

# Implementation

We will first define the interface that will be used by our proxy and real subject.

When we simulate the real behavior of these methods with Playground, these methods return a string, telling us what the code is expected to do. We can ensure what we are coding is correct by checking the message returned by Playground.

The interface will have only two methods: `click()` and `display()`:

```
protocol IAnimation{
  func display() -> String
  func click() -> String
}
```

The `RealSubject` object is represented here with the video class. We implement the interface and display the message according to the action:

```
class Video:IAnimation{
  func click() -> String{
    return ""
  }

  func display()->String{
    return "Display the video"
  }

  func load()->String{
    return "Loading the video"
  }

  func play()->String{
    return "Playing the video"
  }
}
```

The proxy now implements the same interface as the RealSubject object: the IAnimation interface but has the intelligence to create the RealSubject object, here the video object, when needed in the click method:

```
class ScreenShot:IAnimation{
  var video:Video?

  func click() -> String {
    if let video = video {
      return video.play()
    } else {
      video = Video()
      return video!.load()
    }
  }

  func display() -> String {
    if let video = video {
      return video.display()
    } else {
      return "Display the screenshot of the video"
    }
  }
}
```

# Usage

The cool part is to simulate the client.

We first create a new proxy, Screenshot, and then we simulate the operation. We call display from the proxy. As the video is not created or loaded, it is the screenshot that will be displayed.

Then, we simulate a click. We can see that when we call the click method, the video gets loaded. As the video is created and loaded, we call the display method, which informs us that the video is now playing (instead of the screenshot of the video):

```
var animation = ScreenShot()
animation.display()
animation.click()
animation.display()
```

The result in Playground is as follows:

```
ScreenShot
"Display the screenshot of the video"
"Loading the video"
"Display the video"
```

 Use the proxy pattern when you have objects, which are as follows:

- Expensive to create
- Need access control
- Access remote sites
- Need to perform some actions whenever they are accessed

Also, use the proxy pattern when you want to:

- Create objects only when their operations are requested
- Perform checks or housekeeping on objects whenever accessed
- Have a local object that will refer to a remote object
- Implement access rights on objects when their operations are requested

# The bridge pattern

Remember that, at the beginning of the chapter, we discussed dynamic composition that allows you to change the implementation of an object at runtime. The bridge pattern is another structural pattern that allows this.

# Roles

The bridge pattern decouples an abstraction from its implementation. This means that this pattern separates the implementation of an object from its representation and interface.

Thus, firstly, the implementation can fully be encapsulated, and secondly, the implementation and representation can independently change, without having any constraints between them.

This pattern can be used:

- To avoid a strong link between the object representation and its implementations
- To avoid any impact between the interaction of the objects and their clients when the implementations of objects are modified
- To allow the representation of objects and their implementations to keep their extension capability by creating new subclasses
- To avoid to obtain very complex classes hierarchies

# Design

In the class diagram of the bridge pattern, the separation between the abstraction and the implementation is very well represented — notice the left-hand side and right-hand side of the following diagram:

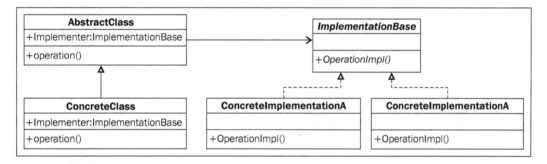

# Participants

The bridge pattern uses a minimum of four participants:

- The `AbstractClass` represents the domain objects. This class contains the interface used by clients and contains a reference to an object that implements the `Implementation` interface.
- The `ConcreteClass` is the class that implements the methods defined in the `AbstractClass`.

- The `ImplementationBase` class defines the method signature of the concrete implementation classes. The methods defined here differ from the methods of the `Abstract` class. These two sets of methods are different. Generally, methods of the `AbstractClass` are high-level methods, while the methods of the `implementation` class are low-level methods.

- The `ConcreteImplementationA` (B …) classes are concrete classes that realize methods introduced in the `ImplementationBase` interface.

 The `ImplementationBase` interface represents the bridge.

# Collaboration

The operation of `AbstractClass` and its subclasses invokes the methods defined in the `ImplementationBase` interface, which represent the bridge.

# Illustration

We should be able to turn on the light or TV using the same object. Once my code to turn on the light or TV will be implemented in my client, I don't need to modify it if the `ConcreteImplementation` structure changes. Using the bridge pattern, I will use an object that inherits from `AbstractClass`. This object contains a method that the client will consume. This method doesn't turn on the TV, but it calls the method defined in the `ImplementationBase` class; thus, depending on the object that our abstract object uses, it will run the actions that are defined in the `ConcreteImplementation` class, which are represented by the TV or the light.

# Implementation

Given the preceding problem, we will first define the method and a property that contains the object we want to manipulate. This object will implement the `ImplementationBase` interface, which represents the bridge.

The object that will be manipulated by clients will have a `turnOn()` method. This is the only method known by the client:

```
// IAbstractBridge
protocol IAbstractBridge {
  var concreteImpl: ImplementationBase {get set}
  func turnOn()
}
```

Now, we will define the `ImplementationBase` interface. It contains the `run()`
method that each `ConcreteImplementation` class will implement:

```
//Bridge
protocol ImplementationBase {
  func run()
}
```

Our interfaces are now ready; we can create the `RemoteControl` class that our
clients will use. Depending on the object referred in the `concreteImpl` property,
the `turnOn()` method will call the run method of the `concreteImpl` object. To obtain
a reference to the `concreteImpl` object, we will add an argument to the constructor
(`init`) of the `RemoteControl` class:

```
/* Concrete Abstraction */
class RemoteControl: IAbstractBridge {
  var concreteImpl: ImplementationBase

  func turnOn() {
    self.concreteImpl.run()
  }

  init(impl: ImplementationBase) {
    self.concreteImpl = impl
  }
}
```

Finally, we implement our `ImplementationBase` class for the `TV` and `Light`
classes. A `run()` method is needed in each of them. The `run()` method contains
all the needed logic that will permit you to turn on the light or TV. In our example,
we only display a text that indicates the action has been completed:

```
/* Implementation Classes 1 */
class TV: ImplementationBase {
  func run() {
    println("tv turned on");
  }
}

/* Implementation Classes 2 */
class Light: ImplementationBase {
  func run() {
    println("light turned on")
  }
}
```

# Usage

From the client's perspective, we will use our `RemoteControl` abstraction class, pass the final object to the constructor when we want to manipulate (the `Light` or `TV` class), and call the `turnOn()` method of the `RemoteControl` object to execute the action:

```
let tvRemoteControl = RemoteControl(impl: TV())
tvRemoteControl.turnOn()


let lightRemoteControl = RemoteControl(impl: Light())
lightRemoteControl.turnOn()
```

Thanks to Playground, we can now see the live result, which is as follows:

```
class TV: ImplementationBase {
  func run() {
    print("tv turned on");                          "tv turned on\n"
  }
}

/* Implementation Classes 2 */
class Light: ImplementationBase {
  func run() {
    print("light turned on")                        "light turned on\n"
  }
}

let tvRemoteControl = RemoteControl(impl: TV())     RemoteControl
tvRemoteControl.turnOn()                            RemoteControl

let lightRemoteControl = RemoteControl(impl: Light())  RemoteControl
lightRemoteControl.turnOn()                         RemoteControl
```

We can see two messages on the right-hand side of our Playground file: **tv turned on** and **light turned on**, which means that the `run()` method of each final object has been correctly executed.

# Summary

We discussed the three structural patterns in this chapter: the decorator pattern, the proxy pattern, and the bridge pattern. From a high-level perspective, all of them help you extend classes without using inheritance, but using a dynamic composition of its class hierarchy.

Extending our original class has some impact on our original object except for the proxy pattern where it remains completely unchanged. The decorator pattern that needs to be designed needs to have the original class already developed because every concrete decorator needs to implement an interface based on the original object structure. The bridge pattern is more closely coupled, and there is an understanding that the original object must incorporate considerable references to the rest of the system.

We also discussed all the patterns that rely on rerouting operations. We learned that the rerouting is always done from the new code back to the original.

It is important to note that in real-time applications, where performance is required, the overhead of the time for rerouting the operations might not be acceptable.

In the next chapter, we will continue our discovery of structural patterns with the composite and flyweight patterns, which can be applied to systems that have huge data objects.

# 3
# Structural Patterns – Composite and Flyweight

We have already seen three structural patterns: the decorator, proxy, and bridge patterns that provide us with ways of adding state and behavior dynamically, controlling the creation and access of objects, and keeping specifications and implementations separate. This chapter will now focus on the composite and flyweight patterns that are designed to facilitate the manipulation of a group of objects or large number of small objects. The composite is often used and we can also make use of the flyweight pattern.

The flyweight pattern efficiently shares the common information present in small objects by helping you reduce the memory consumption or storage requirements when many values are duplicated.

In this chapter, we will discuss the following topics:

- The composite pattern
- The flyweight pattern

The objectives of these two new structural patterns are described in the following table:

| Pattern | Objective |
| --- | --- |
| The composite pattern | This pattern allows you to compose objects into tree structures and treat the group of objects as an instance of an object. |
| The flyweight pattern | This pattern allows you to manage huge number of objects by instantiating them on the fly to improve the performance efficiently. |

# The composite pattern

This pattern is very often used to manipulate a group of objects. Swift, like many other languages already makes use of the composite pattern in its internal structure. For example, in the case of the UIView class available in the cocoa framework, which defines a common behavior of an app layout. Then, individuals view objects in the view hierarchy can be leaf nodes (such as labels) or composites that have collections of other views (such as table view controllers).

## Roles

This pattern permits you to treat single components and a group of components in the same way by providing a structured hierarchy of objects. It allows you to build structures of objects in the form of trees that contain both compositions of objects and individual objects as nodes.

Using this pattern, we can create complex trees and treat them as a whole or as parts. Operations can be applied to the whole or the parts too.

We generally find the add, remove, display, find, and group operations in the Composite class.

This pattern can be used when:

- It is necessary to have a composition hierarchy in a system
- Clients need to be ignored if they are working with composites objects

## Design

The generic UML class diagram is represented in the following figure:

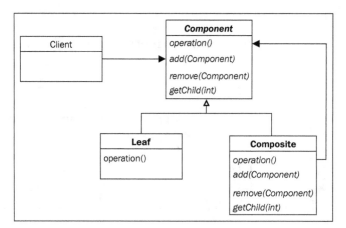

# Participants

The participants of this pattern are as follows:

- Component: This is an abstract class that introduces an object's interface of the composition, implements common methods, and defines the method signature that manages the addition or deletion of components.

- Leaf: This is a concrete class that defines the behavior of the elements in the composition. It implements the operations that the Composite class supports. A Leaf class does not have its own components.

- Composite: This is a concrete class that defines the behavior of the components that have children and store the child components. It implements the Leaf class-related operations. This class has an aggregation of the Component class.

- Client: This class uses the component's interface to manipulate the objects in the composition.

Composite contains components. Components can be Leaf or Composite. It is indeed recursive. A composite holds a set of children; these children may be other composites or leaf elements.

# Collaboration

A client sends a request to the leaf throughout the Component interface.

When a component receives a request, it reacts depending on its class. If the component is a leaf, then it will treat the request itself.

If the component is a composite, it will first treat on itself, then it will send a message to each of its child, which in turn will execute a treatment too. Then, when every child completes their treatment, the composite will execute the last treatment.

# Illustration

Our company has an online catalog of **Video on demand (VOD)**. All our movies are categorized by genre. As this is a pay-per-view system, each of our videos will have a price, name, and small description.

Now, we want to easily manipulate the display of our full catalog using this new pattern. The following schema represents the organization of our catalog:

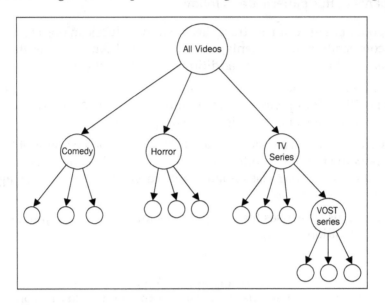

## Implementation

So, it's time for us to apply the generic design of the composite pattern to our case. First, we will redesign our pattern according to our scenario in order to understand what we need to do, as shown in the following diagram:

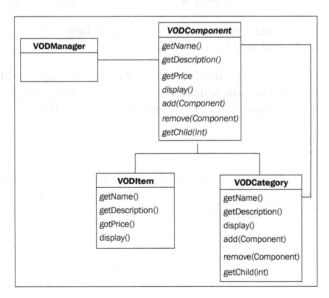

The VODManager class will use the VODComponent interface to access the VOD categories and VOD items. The VODComponent class is our abstract class that will provide the default implementation of the defined methods. The VODItem class will only override the methods that make sense. The VODCategory class will also override methods that make sense, including a way to add the new VODItem and VODCategory objects. After reorganizing our pattern, we are now ready to implement our solution.

# Implementation of the VODComponent

First, we create our abstract class, which both VODItem and VODCategory will inherit form. This class will provide the interface for the leaf nodes and composite nodes. Swift doesn't support an abstract class; nevertheless, nothing should prevent us from implementing the default behavior onto our methods, such as informing that a method is not supported using an **assert**. An assert will just inform us that if it is used in an inappropriate class, then the method will not be supported. We could write our "fake" abstract class like this:

```
// Abstract Class

class VODComponent {

  func add(vodComponent: VODComponent) {
    assert(false, "This method is not supported")
  }

  func remove(vodComponent: VODComponent) {
    assert(false, "This method is not supported")
  }

  func getName() -> String {
    assert(false, "This method is not supported")
  }

  func getDescription() -> String {
    assert(false, "This method is not supported")
  }

  func getPrice() -> Double {
    assert(false, "This method is not supported")
  }

  func getChild(i:Int) -> VODComponent {
```

```
      assert(false, "This method is not supported")
   }

   func display() {
      assert(false, "This method is not supported")
   }
}
```

# Implementation of the VODItem leaf

Our component class is ready; a default behavior is available for each method.
We can now implement our VODItem class. It is a leaf class in the composite
diagram and implements the behavior of the elements of the composite:

```
class VODItem: VODComponent {
   private var name: String!
   Private var description: String!
   private var price: Double!

   init(name:String!, description:String!, price:Double!){
      self.name = name
      self.description = description
      self.price = price
   }

   override func getName() -> String {
      return name!
   }

   override func getDescription() -> String {
      return description!
   }

   override func getPrice() -> Double {
      return price!
   }

   override func display() {
      print(" \(name!), \(price!),  ----  \(description!)")
   }
}
```

See how I have defined the private variables with !. This means that the values of these variables cannot be nil after initialization. This is true because we added a constructor (the init method) where all our arguments must be passed to initialize our private fields.

Then, we override only methods that interest us. The Add/Remove and GetChild methods don't need to be overridden here; this will be done in the composite class.

To ensure that each name, description, and price has a value, we added an exclamation mark to unwrap it.

It is now time to implement our composite category class. We will call this composite class: VODCategory. It will hold VODItems or VODCategory. You'll see that again we will override only methods that interest us in this class. The getPrice() method will not interest us as it doesn't make sense.

# Implementation of the VODCategory composite

The first shot of the VodCategory class could be written as follow:

```
class VODCategory: VODComponent{
  var vodComponents = [VODComponent]()
  private var name: String!
  private var description: String!

  init(name:String!, description:String!) {
    self.name = name
    self.description = description
  }

  override func add(vodComponent: VODComponent) {
    vodComponents.append(vodComponent)
  }

  override func remove(vodComponent: VODComponent) {
    vodComponents.remove(vodComponent)
  }

  override func getChild(i:Int) -> VODComponent {
    return vodComponents[i]
  }
```

```
    override func getName() -> String {
      return name!
    }

    override func getDescription() -> String {
      return description!
    }

    override func display() {
      print(" \(name!),  \(description!) \r\n --------------")
    }
  }
```

Well, as with VODComponent, we override the methods that interest us. As we can have any number of VODComponent, we add an array of type VODComponent to hold them.

We added the Add, Remove, and GetChild methods. The Add method will allow us to add an item, category, or subcategory. We can also remove it and return a VODComponent class based on its index.

Again, we can add a name and description to our composite that will be displayed when the display() method will be invoked.

Let's take a look at the following code:

```
    override func remove(vodComponent: VODComponent) {
      vodComponents.remove(vodComponent)
    }
```

If you write it like the preceding code, you'll get an error because Swift doesn't provide a remove method for the Array type.

It's time to make some modifications in our implementation and introduce you to the use of extensions.

Our problem is that we want to be able to remove an object of the type VODComponent to our vodComponents array using a method called remove (or anything else), where we pass an object that represents the object we want to remove from the list.

If we check the available method when the auto-completion is displayed, we do not see any method that can help us in this purpose, as shown in the following screenshot:

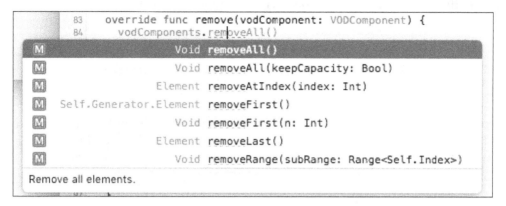

In *Chapter 2, Structural Patterns – Decorator, Proxy, and Bridge,* you could have used the decorator pattern to add such methods to the `Array` type; you can also propose to simply add a method to the class that will test all the elements in the array by comparing them one by one, and if they are identical, remove them from the list.

What we want is something that can be reused and generic. For this, Swift has `extension`. This permits you to add a behavior to a class very easily. Let's do it by adding a `remove` method to the type `Array`.

The extension must not be added to a class. Indeed, extensions are global. If you add extensions to an OS X or iOS project, you'll generally add them to a dedicated Swift file.

Here is our extension:

```
extension Array {
  mutating func remove <T: Equatable> (object: T) {
    for i in (self.count-1).stride(through: 0, by: -1) {
      if let element = self[i] as? T {
        if element == object {
          self.removeAtIndex(i)
        }
      }
    }
  }
}
```

As this function modifies the instance of the `Array` type and its properties, we mark this function as mutating. Then, we start from the end of the list and compare the elements that we want to find in the current elements of the list:

```
if let element = self[i] as? T {
  if element == object {
    self.removeAtIndex(i)
  }
}
```

Again, here there are some tricky things to do to make this code without any error. This function tells that we want that `Array` of type `T` must implement `Equatable` (is said with `remove <T: Equatable>`) to be able to make the comparison:

```
if element == object {
```

Therefore, we need to modify our abstract class, telling that our class implements the `Equatable` protocol:

```
class VODComponent : Equatable {

  func add(vodComponent:VODComponent){
    assert(false, "This method is not supported")
  }
```

Of course, adding this protocol modifies our class diagram a little, but no matter. By implementing this protocol we are telling that elements of type `VODComponent` can be compared using `==` and `!=`.

If this is not completed, then we need to implement this protocol, so the best way to do this is by making a global function outside any class:

```
// GLOBAL Func
func ==(left: VODComponent, right: VODComponent) -> Bool {
  return left === right
}
```

 The `===` operator tells us whether the instances of the two components are identical or not.

So, now, all the code required for this class is written; the `remove` method is available and works perfectly.

Some improvements need to be added to our class to fully complete the implementation of the composite.

Have you seen how we implemented the `display` method in our composite (`VODCategory`)? Indeed, the `display()` method of the composite only displays the information about itself, but it must invoke the `display()` method of each element that is contained in the composite. To do this, we will simply add a small part of the code that will iterate all elements that the composite contains in its array by adding a call to their respective `display()` methods.

Let's change the `display()` method of the `VODCategory` class to add an iteration to all our elements:

```
//VODCategory
class VODCategory:VODComponent{


    ...

    override func display() {
       print(" \(name!),  \(description!) \r\n ---------------")
       for e in vodComponents{
           e.display()
       }
    }
}
```

So, we iterate over each element of the array using `for ... in` and call the `display()` method of each element.

# Usage

All our classes are now ready and it's time to see how we can use this pattern in our client to test all of this.

We first prepare our `VODManager` class:

```
class VODManager{
   var catalog:VODComponent

   init(vod: VODComponent) {
       catalog = vod
   }

   func displayCatalog() {
       catalog.display()
   }
}
```

Then, we write our test code:

```
//USAGE
let horrorCategory = VODCategory(name: "Horror", description:
   "Horror movies category")
let tvSeriesCategory = VODCategory(name: "TV Series", description:
   "TV Series category")
let comedyCategory = VODCategory(name: "Comedy", description:
   "Comedy category")
let voSTTvSeries = VODCategory(name: "VOSTSeries", description:
   "VOST TV Series sub category")

let allVODComponents = VODCategory(name: "All VOD", description:
   "All vod components")
let vodManager = VODManager(vod: allVODComponents)

allVODComponents.add(horrorCategory)
allVODComponents.add(tvSeriesCategory)
allVODComponents.add(comedyCategory)

tvSeriesCategory.add(voSTTvSeries)

horrorCategory.add(VODItem(name: "Scream", description: "Scream
   movie", price: 9.99))
horrorCategory.add(VODItem(name: "Paranormal Activity",
   description: "Paranormal Activity movie", price: 9.99))
horrorCategory.add(VODItem(name: "Blair Witch Project",
   description: "Blair Witch movie", price: 9.99))

tvSeriesCategory.add(VODItem(name: "Game of thrones S1E1",
description: "Game of thrones Saison 1 episode 1", price: 1.99))
tvSeriesCategory.add(VODItem(name: "Deadwood", description:
   "Deadwood Saison 1 episode 1", price: 1.99))
tvSeriesCategory.add(VODItem(name: "Breaking Bad", description:
   "Breaking Bad Saison 1 Episode 1 " , price: 1.99))

voSTTvSeries.add(VODItem(name: "Doc Martin", description: "Doc
   Martin French serie Saison 1 Episode 1", price: 1.99))
voSTTvSeries.add(VODItem(name: "Camping Paradis", description:
   "Camping Paradis French serie Saison 1 Episode 1", price: 1.99))

comedyCategory.add(VODItem(name: "Very Bad Trip", description:
   "Very Bad Trip Movie", price: 9.99))
```

```
comedyCategory.add(VODItem(name: "Hot Chick", description: "Hot
  Chick Movie", price: 9.99))
comedyCategory.add(VODItem(name: "Step Brothers", description:
  "Step Brothers Movie", price: 9.99))
comedyCategory.add(VODItem(name: "Bad teacher", description: "Bad
  Teacher Movie", price: 9.99))


vodManager.displayCatalog()
```

We need to prepare all our components. So, first, we prepare our tree category and then we add items to the good category.

At the end of the script, we call the `vodManager.displayCatalog()` method that will invoke the `display` method of all the components.

So, why don't we see something interesting in Playground? In fact, we have some clues that tell us that the code has been properly executed.

On the right-hand side of the screen, we can see the number of times a method has been called, as shown in the following screenshot:

```
63    override func display() -> String {
64       return " \(name!), \(price!),   ----  \(description!)"         (12 times)
65    }
```

```
99    override func display() -> String {
100      var text = " \(name!), \(description!) \r\n              (5 times)
         ------------------"
101      for e in vodComponents{
102         text += "\r\n\(e.display()) \r\n"                           (16 times)
103      }
104      return text                                                    (5 times)
105   }
```

However, we will modify this a little bit to get something more accurate for our test. We will modify each `display()` method by adding the string `return` type and replace the `print` statement with a `return` statement that contains the string to be returned:

```
override func display() -> String{
   return " \(name!), \(price!),   ----  \(description!)"
}
```

You need to change the `display()` method of the `VODComponent`, `VODItem`, and `VODCategory` classes.

For `VODCategory`, you need to modify it like the following code so that it is easily readable:

```
override func display() -> String{
    var text = " \(name!),  \(description!) \r\n ----------------"
    for e in vodComponents {
        text += "\r\n\(e.display()) \r\n"
    }
    return text
}
```

For `VODManager`, you need to simply add the return type and replace `print` with `return`:

```
func displayCatalog() -> String{
    return catalog.display()
}
```

Finally, move the `tvSeriesCategory.add(voSTTvSeries)` line in the *Usage* section (marked with a comment : // USAGE) of the Playground file ( just before the `vodManager.display()` line; this will make our result easier to read.

Now, you will see something on the right-hand side just after the `vodManager.display()` line:

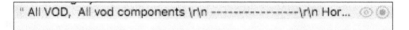

Click on the Eye icon on the right-hand side of the screen. You'll see the result of our `vodManager.display()` invocation:

```
All VOD,  All vod components
        ----------------
   Horror,  Horror movies category
        ----------------
   Scream, 9.99,  ----  Scream movie

Paranormal Activity, 9.99,  ----  Paranormal Activity movie

 Blair Witch Project, 9.99,  ----  Blair Witch movie


        TV Series,  TV Series category
             ----------------
Game of thrones S1E1, 1.99,  ----  Game of thrones Saison 1 episode 1

    Deadwood, 1.99,  ----  Deadwood Saison 1 episode 1

    Breaking Bad, 1.99,  ----  Breaking Bad Saison 1 Episode 1

    VOSTSeries,  VOST TV Series sub category
             ----------------
   Doc Martin, 1.99,  ----  Doc Martin French serie Saison 1 Episode 1

Camping Paradis, 1.99,  ----  Camping Paradis French serie Saison 1
                          Episode 1



        Comedy,  Comedy category
             ----------------
   Very Bad Trip, 9.99,  ----  Very Bad Trip Movie

    Hot Chick, 9.99,  ----  Hot Chick Movie

 Step Brothers, 9.99,  ----  Step Brothers Movie

   Bad teacher, 9.99,  ----  Bad Teacher Movie
                      ...
```

Notice that the `display()` method of the composite or leaf is called recursively. The items are organized depending on the categories that we have added them to. In the preceding screenshot, we can see that after `Horror VODCategory` is called, all horror movies (`VODItem`) that we defined are displayed, then it continues with the TV series that also contain a `VOST TV Series` subcategory, and so on.

This concludes our discovery of the composite pattern.

# The flyweight pattern

This pattern can be used when the system needs to deal with a large number of similar objects. Instead of creating each element one by one, this pattern permits you to reuse an object that shares the same data.

## Roles

The flyweight pattern is used to reduce the memory and resource usage of complex models that contain many hundreds and thousands of similar objects by reducing the number of objects created. It tries to reuse similar existing objects or creates a new one when no match is found.

This pattern can be used when:

- We need to manipulate a lot of small similar objects
- The cost (the memory/execution time) of this manipulation is high

## Design

The following class diagram represents the generic structure of the pattern:

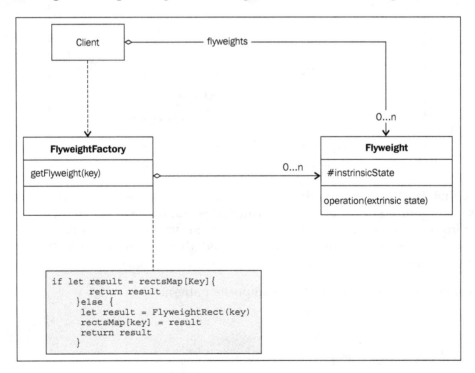

# Participants

There are three participants to the flyweight pattern, as follows:

- `Flyweight`: This declares an interface that contains an intrinsic state and implements methods. These methods can receive and act on the extrinsic state of the flyweights.
- `FlyweightFactory`: This factory creates and manages a flyweight's objects. It assures that the flyweight is shared, thanks to the method that it returns a reference to the flyweight.
- `Client`: This contains references to the used flyweight. It also contains the extrinsic state of these flyweights.

**The extrinsic state**: This is the state that belongs to the context of the object (external) or unique to that instance.

**The intrinsic state**: This is the state that belongs to the flyweight object and should be permanent or immutable (internal).

# Collaboration

Clients do not create the flyweight by themselves, but they use the `FlyweightFactory` method that guarantees the sharing of flyweights.

When a client invokes a method of a flyweight, it needs to send its extrinsic state.

# Illustration

Suppose that we want to display 200000 rectangles on a 1024 x 768 screen. These rectangles are generated randomly; they can have a random color from a list of 10 different colors.

We need to reduce the time taken to execute the function and use as less memory as possible.

# Implementation

In this example, we will use an `XCTest` project with the `XCTest` framework and instrument tool to illustrate how this pattern will help us reduce the memory consumption.

First, open the project called `Flyweight Pattern_Demo1` that you will find in the source code folder of this chapter.

Go to the Xcode project named `FlyweightPattern_Demo1Tests` and click on the `FlyweightPattern_Demo1Tests.swift` file, as shown in the following screenshot:

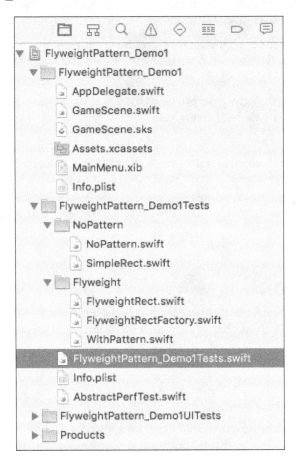

In this file, you'll see the different test methods that are already implemented. Before starting with the implementation of our flyweight pattern, let's see what we currently have.

We already have an abstract class called `AbstractPerfTest` that contains some already defined properties, fields, and methods:

```swift
class AbstractPerfTest {

  let colors:[SKColor] = [
    SKColor.yellowColor(),
    SKColor.blackColor(),
    SKColor.cyanColor(),
    SKColor.whiteColor(),
    SKColor.blueColor(),
    SKColor.brownColor(),
    SKColor.redColor(),
    SKColor.greenColor(),
    SKColor.grayColor(),
    SKColor.purpleColor()
  ]

  let sks = SKScene()
  let view = SKView(frame: NSRect(x: 0, y: 0, width: 1024, height:
  768))

  let maxRectWidth = 100
  let maxRectHeight = 100

  //must be overriden
  func run(){
    preconditionFailure("Must be overriden")
  }


  // - MARK generate Rect Height and Width
  func generateRectWidth() -> Int{
    return Int(arc4random_uniform(UInt32(maxRectWidth)))
  }

  func generateRectHeight() -> Int{
    return Int(arc4random_uniform(UInt32(maxRectHeight)))
  }

  // - MARK generate Position X and Y
  func generateXPos() -> Int{
```

```
    return Int(arc4random_uniform(UInt32(view.bounds.size.width)))
  }

  func generateYPos() -> Int{
    return
    Int(arc4random_uniform(UInt32(view.bounds.size.height)))
  }
}
```

There is another class called `NoPattern` that inherits from this abstract class and overrides the run method:

```
import Foundation
// Inherits from our AbstractPerfTest class
// which contains default methods and init
class NoPattern:AbstractPerfTest {
  // Execute the test
  override func run(){
    var j:Int = 0
    for _ in 1...NUMBER_TO_GENERATE {
      let idx = Int(arc4random_uniform(UInt32(self.colors.count-
      1)))

      let rect = SimpleRect(color: self.colors[idx])
      rect.display(generateXPos(), yPos: generateYPos(), width:
      generateRectWidth(), height: generateRectHeight())
      j++
    }
    print("\(j) rects generated")
  }
}
```

The `SimpleRect` class is defined in the `SimpleRect.swift` file of the `NoPattern` group folder. It is an object defined by a color, *x* and *y* position, width, and height.

I will not comment too much on the `NoPattern` class, but what we see here is that the run method of the `NoPattern` class generates NUMBER_TO_GENERATE (set to 100000 by default in the `FlyweightPattern_Demo1Tests.swift` file) rectangles with a random color taken from the list of the colors array (defined in the abstract class). It then generates a position and dimension for each of these rectangles.

Now, let's check the performance of the `run` method.

Come back to the `FlyweightPattern_Demo1Tests.swift` file and check the method named `testSimpleScreenFilling_noFlyWeight()`. Here, the method will execute the code implemented in the `NoPattern` class that, like the name of the method tells us, does not implement the flyweight pattern. The execution time of this method will be used as a baseline to compare the same method but with the implementation of the flyweight pattern.

So, let's execute the test by clicking on the small icon on the left-hand side of the `func testSimpleScreenFilling_noFlyWeight()` function, as shown in the following screenshot:

```
32      //TEST without applying the pattern
33      func testSimpleScreenFilling_noFlyweight() {
34          // This is an example of a performance test case.
35          // it is executed 10 times by default to get an average
36
37          self.measureBlock() {
38              let noPattern = NoPattern()
39              noPattern.run()
40          }
41      }
42
```

We need to ensure that the console is visible in Xcode. While executing, you'll see that the console log with **200000 rects generated** has been repeated 10 times. This proves that our code has generated 2,00,000 rectangles 10 times. By default, the `self.measureBlock` closure is executed 10 times, and it calculates the standard deviation of these 10 executions to obtain an average execution time:

```
200000 rects generated
200000 rects generated
200000 rects generated
200000 rects generated
200000 rects generated
200000 rects generated
200000 rects generated
200000 rects generated
200000 rects generated
200000 rects generated
```

On my MacBook Pro 15 Retina Late 2013, the average time is **0.804** seconds:

```
self.measureBlock() {
    let noPattern = NoPattern()
    noPattern.run()
}
                                          Time: 0.804 sec (5% STDEV)
```

Now, the best part is to refactor our code to reduce the time taken to generate these 2,00,000 rectangles. As you have already seen in the generic structure of the pattern, we will need a few classes to manage our flyweights.

Let's start with our `flyweightRect` class. Note that the `flyweightRect` and `SimpleRect` classes are used in the `NoPattern` class to generate rectangles that are identical.

Therefore, in the following code, you'll find our `FlyweightRect` class with the definition of our rectangle. So, we have a color, $x$ and $y$ position, height, and width of the rectangle.

Note that because I really want to see the gain in performance, I added two fields: `image` and `sprite`. Because the value of these fields have a cost in terms of performance on the instantiation of the class, I added them to show you clearly that the flyweight pattern permits you to reduce the calculation costs (and memory usage) when applied.

We will add a constructor to the intrinsic state as an argument: this will be the color. We will add another `display()` method that will receive extrinsic states as arguments:

```
import SpriteKit
import Foundation

class FlyweightRect {

    var color: SKColor!
    var xPos: Int?
    var yPos: Int?
    var width: Int?
    var height: Int?
    var image: NSImage?
    var sprite: SKSpriteNode?

    //the constructor contains our intrinsic state
    init(color: SKColor) {
```

```
        self.color = color
        self.image = NSImage()
        self.sprite = SKSpriteNode()
    }

    func display(xPos: Int, yPos: Int, width: Int, height: Int){
        self.xPos = xPos
        self.yPos = yPos
        self.width = width
        self.height = height
    }

    func description() -> String  {
        return "rect position: \(self.xPos), \(self.yPos) : dimension:
        \(self.width), \(self.height)  : color: \(self.color)"
    }
}
```

Once our flyweight is defined, we can now prepare our `FlyweightFactory` object. Remember that this factory will first check if we already have a rectangle that is similar to the new one that we want to position on the screen; if it is not similar, then it will create a new one:

```
import SpriteKit
import Foundation

class FlyweightRectFactory{
    internal static var rectsMap = Dictionary<SKColor,
    FlyweightRect>()

  static func getFlyweightRect(color:SKColor) -> FlyweightRect{
    if let result = rectsMap[color]{
       return result
    } else { // if nil add it to our dictionnary
      let result = FlyweightRect(color: color)
      rectsMap[color] = result
      return result
    }
  }
}
```

We declare a static `rectsMap` variable of the type `Dictionary` that will contain our shared objects and manage their existence. The dictionary `Key` will contain a `Color` object.

Then, we define a static method called `getFlyweightRect` that will return a `FlyweightRect` class.

As `rectMaps[color]` returns `nil`, we unwrap the optional with a `if let` statement. If it is not `nil`, we return the result; otherwise, we create a new flyweight with the appropriate color, add it to our dictionary, and return the result.

> In the `FlyweightPattern_Demo1.swift` file, you'll find several test methods that test the response time of the factory depending on the type of the object that manages our flyweights. In the project, I tested the performance of the object that manages our flyweights using the `Dictionary<SKColor, FlyweightRect>`, `NSMutableDictionary`, and `NSCache` types.

The complete code of the `FlyweightRectFactory.swift` file is as follows:

```swift
import SpriteKit
import Foundation

class FlyweightRectFactory {

  internal static var rectsMap = Dictionary<SKColor,
  FlyweightRect>()
  internal static var rectsMapNS = NSMutableDictionary()
  internal static var rectsMapNSc = NSCache()


  static func getFlyweightRect(color:SKColor) -> FlyweightRect{
    if let result = rectsMap[color]{
        return result
    }else {        let result = FlyweightRect(color: color)
      rectsMap[color] = result
      return result
    }
  }



  static func getFlyweightRectWithNS(color: SKColor) ->
  FlyweightRect{

    let result = rectsMapNS[color.description]
```

```
    if result == nil {
      let flyweight= FlyweightRect(color: color)
      rectsMapNS.setObject(flyweight, forKey: color.description)
      return flyweightas FlyweightRect
    }else {
      return result as! FlyweightRect
    }

  }

  static func getFlyweightRectWithNSc(color: SKColor) ->
  FlyweightRect{

    let result = rectsMapNSc.objectForKey(color.description)

    if result == nil {
      let flyweight= FlyweightRect(color: color)
      rectsMapNSc.setObject(flyweight, forKey:color.description)
      return flyweight as FlyweightRect
    }else {
      return result as! FlyweightRect
    }
  }
}
```

# Usage

Using our pattern is extremely easy. You need to check the `run()` method of the `WithPattern.swift` file:

```
class WithPattern:AbstractPerfTest{
  //Execute the test
  override func run(){
    var j:Int = 0
    for _ in 1...NUMBER_TO_GENERATE{
      let idx = Int(arc4random_uniform(UInt32(self.colors.count-
      1)))
      let rect =
      FlyweightRectFactory.getFlyweightRect(self.colors[idx])
      rect.display(generateXPos(), yPos: generateYPos(), width:
      generateRectWidth(), height: generateRectHeight())
      j++
    }
```

```
    print("\(j) rects generated")
    //print("nb Map: \(FlyweightRectFactory.rectsMap.count)")
}
```

We will simply make a loop to create 200000 `FlyweightRect` objects (`NUMBER_TO_ GENERATE` is a constant defined at the top of the `FlyweightPattern_Demo1Tests. swift` file).

The `WithPattern` class written in the preceding does the following:

1. We first generate a random number that returns a value that will correspond to the index of a color available in the colors array (defined in the `AbstractPerfTest.swift` file).

2. Then, we tell the factory to return a flyweight with the appropriate color.

3. Then, we generate the extrinsic state (*x* position, *y* position, width, and height).

4. Once the loop is complete, we display the number of generated rectangles.

## Performance results

To check the performance, there is an `XCTest` class available in the project with the `self.measureblock` closure that allows us to measure the performance of our block.

To launch all the tests available in the project, click on the **Show the Test navigator** button on the left-hand side, as shown in the following screenshot:

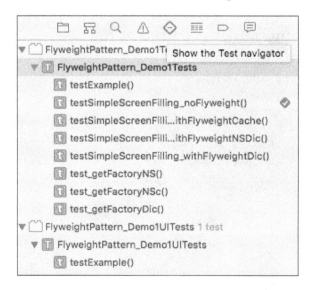

Then, click on the play button that is visible on the right-hand side of the highlighted line:

After a few seconds, all the tests would have been run and you can now check your performance results.

Come back to the `FlyweightPattern_Demo1Tests.swift` file and check the end of each `measureblock()` method. This is the result with the flyweight pattern using a dictionary. You can see that it took an average of 0.247 seconds to generate 200000 rectangles, as shown in the following screenshot. You'll see a text with `Time xxxx` written; this is the average time taken to execute this block:

```
//Dictionnary
func testSimpleScreenFilling_withFlyweightDic() {
    // This is an example of a performance test case.
    // it is executed 10 times by default to get an average

    self.measureBlock() {
        let withPattern = WithPattern()
        withPattern.run()
    }                                          Time: 0.247 sec (9% STDEV)
}
```

As compared to an average of **0.877** seconds without using the pattern:

```
//TEST without applying the pattern
func testSimpleScreenFilling_noFlyweight() {
    // This is an example of a performance test case.
    // it is executed 10 times by default to get an average

    self.measureBlock() {
        let noPattern = NoPattern()
        noPattern.run()
    }                                          Time: 0.877 sec (6% STDEV)
}
```

After reviewing the results, you'll see that generating rectangles are better when (best performance first):

- The flyweight pattern with a `Dictionary` object is used to manage our shared objects
- The flyweight pattern with a `NSDictionary` object is used to manage our shared objects
- The flyweight pattern with a `NSCache` object is used to manage our shared objects
- No pattern is applied

In this example, we can say that generating 200000 `FlyweightRect` objects is 3,55 times faster than without using the pattern.

The test project proves that Swift is faster than Objective-C and `NSCache`, which are encapsulated.

The `NSDictionary` object will have its own logic while handling the cache. It can create more objects inside its own hidden code structure, so it's slower than the `NSDictionary` object.

# Summary

In this chapter, you learned how to deal with structures of multiple objects. The composite pattern allows you to access and alter data structures in a uniform way, whereas the flyweight pattern is a more accurate way to save the memory space or time spent in calculation when they are multiple similar objects.

A flyweight pattern is useful with other patterns to keep data as small as possible. The composite pattern is useful in combination with other patterns to manage the data structure. The composite pattern can use a flyweight pattern, but the inverse will not.

In this chapter, I tried to present you with something different; using the `XCTest` framework, to test the performance of our pattern. If you want to dive deeper, you can try to see the difference in the memory allocation using the instrument tools provided in Xcode.

In the next chapter, we will continue with the discovery of our structural patterns by learning what the adapter and facade patterns are.

# 4
# Structural Patterns – Adapter and Facade

In this chapter, we will discuss two new structural patterns: the adapter and facade patterns. We will focus on the adapter pattern that joins together types that were not designed to work with each other. Then, we will discuss the facade pattern that simplifies the interface of a set of complex systems.

## The adapter pattern

This pattern is often used when dealing with frameworks, libraries, and APIs to easily "adapt" the old and existing interfaces to the new requirements of a program.

## Roles

The adapter pattern converts the interface of another existing class into an interface waited by the existing clients to allow them to work together. Thanks to this pattern, you can integrate components for which you normally cannot modify the source code and things that often appear with the use of a framework.

Note that you should avoid using this pattern if you already have source code access to the component.

# Design

The generic class diagram of the pattern is as follows:

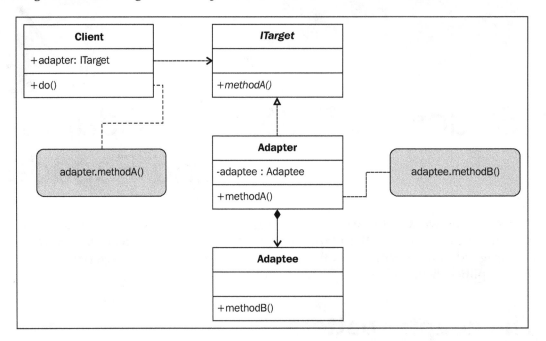

# Participants

In the preceding diagram, you can see the four participants of this pattern:

- ITarget: This introduces the method signature of the object through this interface
- Client: The client interacts with objects that implement the ITarget interface
- Adapter: This class implements the method of the ITarget interface and invokes the method of the adapted object
- Adaptee: This is the object for which we need to adapt its interface to make it manipulable by the client

# Collaboration

The client invokes the methodA() adapter that itself invokes the methodB() adapter of the adaptee object.

The following following screenshot represent the organization of our project:

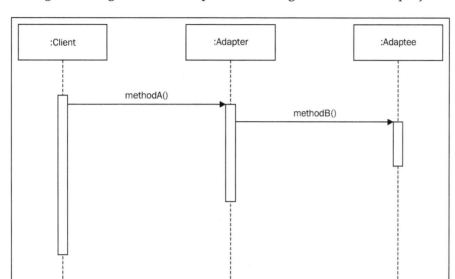

# Illustration

The sales director of your company wants to produce a universal battery charger for mobile phones. This charger can deliver up to 10 volts as output. As the CIO of the company, a member of your development team presents you a first prototype of the charger.

In this chapter, I created a new OS X Command Line Tool project that you'll find in the `first_prototype` folder, and I have named it `ChargerPrototype`.

## Implementing our first prototype

Our project is organized as follows:

- The `Interfaces` folder contains the definition of the methods that the client will invoke to charge the phone
- The `PhonePrototype.swift` file is a class that defines our test phone and implements the `IChargeable` protocol

The result is as follows:

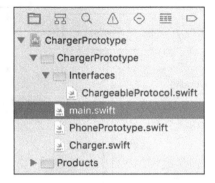

The `ChargeableProtocol` interface is a simple protocol that defines the signature of the `charge` method:

```
import Foundation

protocol ChargeableProtocol {

    /// This function is called to charge a mobile phone
    ///
    /// Usage:
    ///
    ///     charge(5.5)
    ///
    /// - Parameter volts: voltage needed to charge the battery
    ///
    /// - returns: Void
    func charge(volts: Double)
}
```

Consider that Swift protocols have the same concepts as interfaces.

There are some differences between protocols and Java interfaces, which are as follows:

- Swift protocols can also specify properties that must be implemented (for example, fields)
- Swift protocols need to deal with values/references through the use of the mutating keyword (because protocols can be implemented by structs and classes)

You can combine protocols at any point with the `protocol<>` keyword, for example, declaring a function parameter that must adhere to the A and B protocols, which is as follows:

```
func foo ( var1 : protocol<A, B> ){}
```

Next, we define a `PhonePrototype` class that can be charged using the `ChargeableProtocol` protocol:

```swift
class PhonePrototype: ChargeableProtocol {
  /// This function is called to charge a mobile phone
  ///
  /// Usage:
  ///
  ///     charge(5.5)
  ///
  /// - Parameter volts: voltage needed to charge the battery
  ///
  /// - returns: Void
  func charge(volts: Double) {
    print("Charging our PhonePrototype")
    print("current voltage \(volts)")
  }
}
```

Note the comments added to the code here. With Swift, you can add organized comments that allow you to see the information with a popover (by holding *Alt* + pointing mouse cursor on the swift the method you want usage information). To check the result of how the comment are displayed proceed like this:

1. Open the `Charger.swift` file. This file represents our universal charger.

2. Tap and hold the *Alt* key.

3. Position the mouse `charge` that appears in the `self.phone.charge(volts)` statement. An interrogation point ? will appear.

4. Click on charge.

Then, you will see the following popover, as shown in the following screenshot:

You should consider detailed comments of your functions as best practices. Make sure that all your methods are fully commented. You can check how the popover is well-documented, as follows:

- Use `///` to start documenting your code
- Use `- Parameter parametername: description of the parameter` to describe your parameter
- Use `- returns: type to return` to describe the returned type

 For more information on existing keywords to document your code, you should check out the following website:
`http://ericasadun.com/2015/06/14/swift-header-documentation-in-xcode-7/`.

Your engineers present you the prototype of the charger and it seems to work fine.

After loading the `ChargerPrototype.xcodeproject` file in Xcode, click on run to launch the code.

On the console, you will see the following result:

```
First Prototype
A mobile is plugged
Charging our PhonePrototype
current voltage 10.0
Program ended with exit code: 0
```

All Output ◇

Let's see how the `Charger` class has been implemented:

```
import Foundation

class Charger {
  var phone: ChargeableProtocol!
  let volts = 10.0

  func plugMobilePhone(phone: ChargeableProtocol){
    print("A mobile is plugged")
    self.phone = phone
    self.phone.charge(volts)
  }
}
```

The implementation of the preceding code is quite simple. By reading it line by line we can deduct how it works:

- Our charger contains a reference to a phone. The phone must implement `ChargeableProtocol`. Of course, our universal charger will only communicate with this interface.
- Then, we have a method where we can plug our phone.
- We assign the phone to our reference and call the charge method of the referenced phone.

So, your mobile phone charger works fine with all mobile phone chargers that implement `ChargeableProtocol`.

However, there is a problem. Your charger works fine with all phones that implement `ChargeableProtocol` but not with mobile phones available on the market. Indeed, each mobile phone manufacturer has its own interface to charge its own products.

It is impossible to use our charger with the existing mobile phone! A roof for a company that wants to sell universal mobile phone chargers.

You can plan an urgent meeting with your teams in order to find a solution to avoid the bankruptcy of your company.

Mike, a new developer of your company, proposes a solution: "To make all mobile phones work with our charger, they need to implement `ChargeableProtocol`, but we cannot modify the mobile phones because we do not have the source code. So, we can tell each manufacturer to implement `ChargeableProtocol` on their iPhones."

Kevin, the IT project manager, replies, "Mike, welcome to the company, but your solution is not a good choice. Manufacturers have their own systems and they don't want to change them. And what would we do with the phones that are already sold that don't implement `ChargeableProtocol`?"

Kevin continues, "The problem that we have is not the manufacturers' problem; he doesn't have to adapt their code to make our charger work with their products, it is up to our company to adapt ours. Yes, we must adapt our code."

Mike then asks, "So, how do you want to proceed?"

Kevin replies, "Well, the concept is simple. If you plan a trip to France, the electrical outlet specifications and shapes are not adapted to the ones that we have here in the U.S. I stumbled upon an adapter that I bought from an electrical shop near my home. This adapter accepts the shape and specification of my American cable and the other one that can be plugged into the French electrical outlet because the side plugged in has the same shape and specification as the French one. All transformations between the U.S. and French specifications are done in the adapter itself."

"The problem is the same here. We must adapt our charger, depending on the manufacturer. So, we will have an adapter per mobile phone and continue to have a unique charger."

Julien, the CEO, replies, "Great, Kevin! Let's go now. We must make our universal charger available before Christmas!"

# Implementation

The first thing that we need to do is to prepare our adapter to make it work with our charger. The charger works only with object that implements `ChargeableProtocol`. We will need to implement `ChargeableProtocol` with each adapter that we will create.

Once the side charger "plugged to" adapter is completed by implementing `ChargeableProtocol`, we will add a reference to the mobile phone that the adapter adapts. Our universal charger doesn't manipulate the mobile phone instance; it is the role of the adapter to manipulate it.

Open the `ChargerWithAdapter.xcodeproj` project and check the organization of our code:

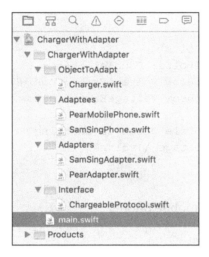

We have grouped our actors in the following three folders:

- `Adaptees`: This contains the component that we must adapt. You can consider this one if you do not have the source code. Remember that you should not use the adapter pattern if you own the source code of the `Adaptee` folder.

- `Adapters`: This contains our adapters depending on the mobile phones that we must charge.

- `Interface`: This contains the interface implemented by our adapters and manipulated by the client.

- `main.swift`: This represents the client: the universal charger.

- `Charger.swift`: This is the object that needs to be adapted.

## Implementation of our adaptees

Let's study two mobiles phones that we need to adapt: the "Pear" mobile phone and "SamSing" mobile phone: Note that in real life, you will not have the source code of the adaptee, the object that needs to be adapted, you'll only work with their known interfaces.

Let's first analyze the SamSing mobile phone:

```swift
import Foundation
class SamSingMobilePhone {

  enum VoltageError: ErrorType {
    case TooHigh
    case TooLow
  }

  ///Accept only 10 volts
  func chargeBattery(volts: Double) throws {
    if volts > 10 { throw VoltageError.TooHigh }
    if volts < 10 { throw VoltageError.TooLow }

    print("SamSing mobile phone is charging")
    print("Current voltage \(volts)")
  }
}
```

Now, let's analyze the Pear mobile phone:

```swift
import Foundation

class PearMobilePhone {

  enum PearVoltageError: ErrorType {
    case NoPower
    case TooLow
    case TooHigh
  }

  ///Accept only 5.5 volts
  func charge(volts: Double) throws {
    guard volts > 0 else { throw PearVoltageError.NoPower}
    if volts > 5.5 { throw PearVoltageError.TooHigh }
    if volts < 5.5 { throw PearVoltageError.TooLow }

    print("Pear mobile phone is charging")
    print ("Current voltage \(volts)")
  }
}
```

These two classes represent our objects that need to be adapted: the first one is the `SamSingMobilePhone` class that has a method called `chargeBattery`. This is the method used by the original charger to charge the SamSing mobile phone.

The second one is the `PearMobilePhone` class that allows the original charger to charge the battery but this one is simply called `charge`. Note that the two mobiles phone need different voltages to be charged.

So what you see here is that our universal charger will need to be adapted to call the `charge` method when the Pear mobile phone is plugged in and call the `chargeBattery` method when the SamSing mobile phone is plugged in.

We will have to make an adapter for each mobile phone type that we want to be able to charge.

As mentioned earlier, you should not have the source code of the `adaptee` object when you use the adapter pattern. The source code is provided here only for demonstration purposes.

Have you checked the source code of our two adaptees? I have voluntary introduced two new Swift keywords that I wish to present you.

First, both classes have an enumeration of possible errors that the charger can handle. The SamSing will throw an error if the voltage is too high or too low; the Pear model can throw the same errors and can throw another one if there is absolutely no power when it is plugged to the charger. As mentioned in the documentation, in Swift, errors are represented by values of type conforming to the `ErrorType` protocol. This is the reason why you see each enumeration implementing the `ErrorType` protocol:

```
enum PearVoltageError: ErrorType {
  case NoPower
  case TooLow
  case TooHigh
}
```

Having this enumeration is not sufficient; we need to handle errors when the `charge` method is called. For this, we need to tell the method to throw an exception.

For this, we simply add the `throw` keyword just before we define the return type, as follows:

```
func chargeBattery(volts:Double) throws {
```

Remember that this function definition is exactly the same as:

```
func charge(volts:Double) throws -> Void {
```

Not providing the return type is equivalent to stating that the return type is of the type `Void`.

Well, once our method is informed that it can handle errors, we still have to raise an error when it is necessary to do so. We make some conditional checks at the beginning of the method, and if something goes wrong, it throws an exception. To raise an exception, we simply use the `throw` keyword just before the `ErrorType` object (implementing the ErrorType protocol) that we want to raise. (Here is a VoltageError):

```
if volts > 10 { throw VoltageError.TooHigh }
if volts < 10 { throw VoltageError.TooLow }
```

As mentioned earlier, the `PearMobilePhone` class raises an error; this is when the method receives 0 voltage from the charger. In this case, the `PearVoltageError.NoPower` value of the `PearVoltageError` enumeration type will be raised.

Let's investigate the `charge` method of the `PearMobilePhone` class:

```
///Accept only 5.5 volts
func charge(volts: Double) throws -> Void {
    guard volts > 0 else { throw PearVoltageError.NoPower}
    if volts > 5.5 { throw PearVoltageError.TooHigh }
    if volts < 5.5 { throw PearVoltageError.TooLow }

    print("Pear mobile phone is charging")
    print("Current voltage \(volts)")
}
```

We see that the two `if` statements check whether the voltage is, superior to 5.5 volts in the first case, and inferior to 5.5 volts in the second case. Each of these `if` statements can throw an error: `TooHigh` or `TooLow`.

Now, let's check how the `NoPower` error is raised:

```
guard volts > 0 else { throw PearVoltageError.NoPower}
```

This statement introduces the new Swift 2 keyword, `guard ... else {`.

The `guard` statement is like an `if` statement. It executes statements depending on the Boolean value of an expression. The condition must be true for the program to continue after the `guard` statement. A `guard` statement always has an `else` clause. The statement in this clause is executed if the expression is not true.

The `guard` statement allows you to perform an early exit when checking conditions.

Something that I really like about `guard` is to be able to use it as follows:

```
guard let unwrappedVar = myVar else {
   return
}
print("myVar : \(unwrappedVar)")
```

With an earlier version of Swift, you would have written something like this:

```
If let unwrappedVar = myVar {
   Print("myVar : \(unwrappedVar"))
}else {
   return
}
//now if you call the print statement below this will not work
//because unwrappedVar is no longer available in this scope.
print("myVar : \(unwrappedVar)")
```

So, come back to our pattern. We have seen that our two mobile phones don't have the same interface, and we now need to create an adapter for each of them, as shown in the following diagram:

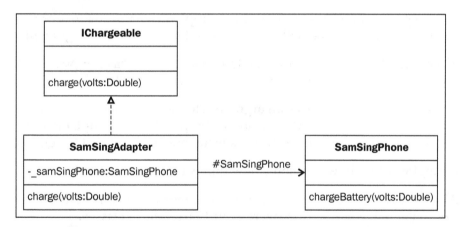

## Implementation of the SamSingAdapter class

In the preceding diagram, we can now code our new adapter that will be able to work with the SamSing mobile phone as follows:

```
import Foundation

class SamSingAdapter: ChargeableProtocol {
```

```
    var samSingPhone: SamSingMobilePhone!

    init(phone: SamSingMobilePhone){
      samSingPhone = phone
    }

    func charge(volts: Double) {
      do {
        print("Adapter started")
        _ = try samSingPhone.chargeBattery(volts)
        print("Adapter ended")
      }catch SamSingMobilePhone.VoltageError.TooHigh{
        print("Voltage is too high")
      }catch SamSingMobilePhone.VoltageError.TooLow{
        print("Voltage is too low")
      }catch{
        print("an error occured")
      }
    }
  }
```

We created a new `SamSingAdapter` class that implements `ChargeableProtocol`. We need to provide a `charge` method that takes the voltage as an argument.

We add a constant called `samSingPhone` that instantiates a `SamSingMobilePhone()` object, which we will use to call its own `chargeBattery` method.

We pass `SamSingMobilePhone` as an argument to the constructor of the adapter to get a reference to the mobile that we want to charge. Then, we implement the code of the charge method. (Remember that this is the only method that the client knows.)

Once again, I want to show you some new things that appear with Swift 2.

Swift 2 introduces the do, `try`, `catch`, and `throw` mechanisms. We already discussed the `throw` statement when we discovered our two `Adaptee` classes.

A method that has the `throw` keyword in its definition is as follows:

```
    func chargeBattery(volts:Double) throws {
```

It must be called using the `try` statement, as this is designed to be clear for developers:

```
      _ = try samSingPhone.chargeBattery(volts)
```

The _ symbol is a wildcard because the `chargeBattery` method of the SamSing mobile doesn't return any value (in fact, it returns `Void`). It is useless to write such a statement:

```
let myVar = try samSingPhone.chargeBattery(volts)
```

Because you want to handle errors that can be thrown by the `chargeBattery` method, this statement must be inside a `do { } catch` block:

```
do {
  print("Adapter started")
  _ = try samSingPhone.chargeBattery(volts)
  print("Adapter ended")
}catch SamSingMobilePhone.VoltageError.TooHigh{
  print("Voltage is too high")
}
//....
```

So, in the `do` block, you'll add the called method that might throw an error, and if you want to handle it, you can catch it in the `catch` blocks:

```
catch SamSingMobilePhone.VoltageError.TooHigh{
  print("Voltage is too high")
}catch SamSingMobilePhone.VoltageError.TooLow{
  print("Voltage is too low")
}catch{
  print("an error occured")
}
```

The `catch` statement will silence all errors and the code will continue to run. If you want to know more about error handling with Swift 2, I recommend that you check out the following website:

https://www.hackingwithswift.com/new-syntax-swift-2-error-handling-try-catch.

Our `SamSingAdapter` class is now ready. We will now do the same with the `PearAdapter` class.

# Implementation of the PearAdapter class

We will proceed in the same way as the `SamSingAdapter` class but with the Pear mobile phone:

```
import Foundation

class PearAdapter: ChargeableProtocol {
```

```
    var pearMobilePhone:PearMobilePhone!

    init(phone: PearMobilePhone){
      pearMobilePhone = phone
    }

    func charge(volts: Double) {
      do {
        print("Adapter started")
        _ = try pearMobilePhone.charge(5.5)
        print("Adapter ended")
      }catch PearMobilePhone.PearVoltageError.TooHigh{
        print("Voltage is too high")
      }catch PearMobilePhone.PearVoltageError.TooLow{
        print("Voltage is too low")
      }catch{
        print("an error occured")
      }
    }
  }
```

Here, the main differences are that we now have a reference to a `PearMobilePhone` object and our `charge` method (that implements `ChargeableProtocol`) calls the `pearMobilePhone.charge` method.

We also need to manage the voltage sent to the phone. An adapter must transform any value to conform to the interface of the adaptee. If we send a very high voltage, our mobile phone will burn and our customers will stop buying our products. So, in our adapter, we set the voltage value sent to the Pear mobile phone to 5.5 volts.

We also catch all the errors that can be thrown by the `charge` method of the `pearMobilePhone` object.

 Swift 2 requires an exhaustive `try/catch` error handling. The last `catch` statement is our default catch-all block.

As we have set the value to 5.5 volts, which is the only voltage accepted by the Pear mobile phone, we will never raise an error, so it is quiet unreadable to have so many catch blocks.

Well, Apple proposes an alternative to you. You can write our adapter like this:

```
    func charge(volts: Double) {
        print("Adapter started")
```

```
        _ = try! pearMobilePhone.charge(5.5)
        print("Adapter ended")
    }
```

The `try!` method allows you to avoid using `do`/`catch` because you are promising that the call will never fail.

We have our universal charger, already ready, two adapters, and two mobile phones to test our charger. Remember that our charger provides 10 volts by default.

Let's write our simple test program in the `main.swift` file:

```
import Foundation

print("*** start test program")
// Create our Charger
let charger = Charger()
print("*** charger ready test program")

//Test 1
//Charge a Pear Mobile Phone
print("Will charge a Pear Mobile Phone")
//1 mobile and adapter creation
let pearPhone = PearMobilePhone()
let pearAdapter = PearAdapter(phone: pearPhone)
//we plug the portable to our charger through the adapter
charger.plugMobilePhone(pearAdapter)

print("*** -")
//Test 2
//Charge a SamSing Mobile Phone
print("Will charge a SamSing Mobile Phone")
//1 mobile and adapter creation
let samSingPhone = SamSingMobilePhone()
let samSingAdapter = SamSingAdapter(phone: samSingPhone)
//we plug the portable to our charger through the adapter
charger.plugMobilePhone(samSingAdapter)

print("*** end test program")
```

I don't think that I need to provide you with more details as the complete code is mentioned here. We prepare our charger, take the first phone, use an appropriate adapter, and then plug the adapter (which is plugged in to our phone too) to the charger. We do the same with the second phone.

Let's run the code and check our result:

```
*** start test program
*** charger ready test program
Will charge a Pear Mobile Phone
A mobile is plugged
Adapter started
Pear mobile phone is charging
Current voltage 5.5
Adapter ended
*** -
Will charge a SamSing Mobile Phone
A mobile is plugged
Adapter started
SamSing mobile phone is charging
Current voltage 10.0
Adapter ended
*** end test program
Program ended with exit code: 0

All Output ◇                                    🗑 | ☐ ☐
```

Well, it doesn't matter what the mobile is; using our appropriate adapter, by default, the charger will send 10 volts, to the adapter, then the adapter will transform this voltage (or not) and call the appropriate charge method on the phone itself.

This concludes the discovery of the adapter pattern.

# The facade pattern

The facade pattern is a simple pattern used to group the interfaces of a group of objects and a unified interface that is easier to use by a client.

## Roles

The facade pattern allows you to provide the operations that might be desirable by a user. The pattern encapsulates the interface of each object that is considered as a low-level interface. To construct the unified interface, we might need to implement some methods that will compose the low-level interfaces:

- It must be used to provide a simple interface of a complex system. The architecture of the system can be composed of several small classes that allow great modularity, but clients don't need such properties. They only need something simple that meets to their needs.

- It can be used to divide the system into subsystems. The façade will be an interface that allows the communication between subsystems.

- It can be also used to encapsulate the implementation of a system toward an external consumer.

# Design

The facade pattern is designed to hide the complexity of a system. Its interface can be entirely new. It must not conform to the existing interface. We can provide several facades to the same system depending on the end user that we have and the functionality that we want to provide to the facade:

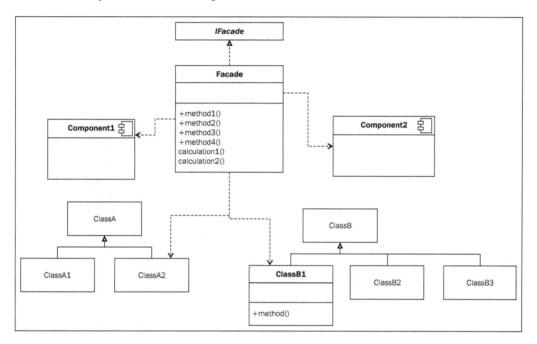

# Participants

The participants of this pattern are as follows:

- Facade and its interface are the abstract parts of the system that are exposed to the clients. This class has some references to classes and components that are part of the system, and they have their methods used by the facade to implement the unified interface.

- The classes and components of the system implement the functionalities of the system and answer requests coming from the facade. They do not need the facade to be able to work.

# Collaboration

Clients communicate with the system through the facade façade. Then, the façade itself invokes classes and components of the system. The facade doesn't only send requests to classes and components of the subsystem. It must also adapt its own interface to the objects and components interfaces, using a specific code to allow communication of objects.

The following sequence diagram describes this case:

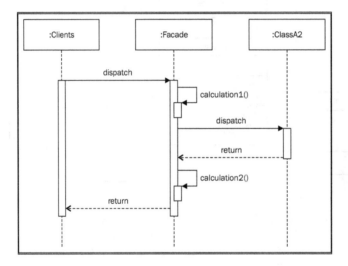

Clients using the facade should not directly access the objects of the system.

# Illustration

We want to provide a simple interface to provide our clients with an easy way to find hotels near an input address and corresponding to some criteria (such as the number of stars.)

In our company, we have a subsystem that provides a catalog of hotels that includes their locations and number of stars for each of them.

We already have a FindPoi Webservice that can search for a hotel near a location point (latitude and longitude), which uses some criteria: the maximum distance to search and the numbers of stars we want.

As you can see, the service needs a location point, which means that we pass an object with a latitude and longitude.

As the consumer of our facade will only tell us its real address, we need services that will geocode the address to a GPS point with a latitude and longitude.

The sequence diagram shows you what we will do to provide our simplified interface:

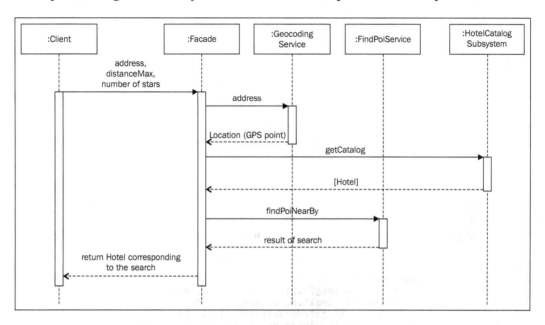

Open the Xcode project called `FacadePattern` and the `main.swift` file. This file represents a client that will consume our facade.

Our facade is, in fact, a service that allows a client to search for a hotel near the location that is sent as an input that has two criteria: `distanceMax` and number of stars for the hotel.

This is how the service will be called:

```
var results = svcFacadeFindHotel.findHotel(myAdress, distanceMax:
    2.0, stars: 4)
```

The complete code of the client is as follows:

```
import Foundation


//I am a consumer of the service
// my addess is
```

```
// 1 infinite Loop
// Cupertino, CA 95014

let svcFacadeFindHotel = ServiceFindHotelNearBy()

let myAdress = " 1 Infinite Loop Cupertino, CA 95014 USA"
var results = svcFacadeFindHotel.findHotel(myAdress, distanceMax:
  2.0, stars: 4)

print("*** RESULTS ")
print("Their is \(results?.count) results :")

if let results = results {
  for var h in results{
    print("Hotel latitude:\(h.location.latitude)
    longitude:\(h.location.longitude), stars: \(h.stars)")
  }
}
```

We open a connection for our `ServiceFindHotelNearBy` service. We tell what our current address is and then display the results if any. Here, we have 125 results (from 1,000 generated in the `HotelCatalog` object):

```
*** RESULTS
Their is Optional(94) results :
Hotel latitude:Optional(-17.0) longitude:Optional(9.0), stars: 4
Hotel latitude:Optional(-44.0) longitude:Optional(-23.0), stars: 4
Hotel latitude:Optional(-1.0) longitude:Optional(-5.0), stars: 4
Hotel latitude:Optional(-22.0) longitude:Optional(8.0), stars: 4
Hotel latitude:Optional(-5.0) longitude:Optional(-25.0), stars: 4
Hotel latitude:Optional(5.0) longitude:Optional(-33.0), stars: 4
Hotel latitude:Optional(-30.0) longitude:Optional(-14.0), stars: 4
Hotel latitude:Optional(-34.0) longitude:Optional(-11.0), stars: 4
Hotel latitude:Optional(-35.0) longitude:Optional(0.0), stars: 4
Hotel latitude:Optional(-11.0) longitude:Optional(-31.0), stars: 4
Hotel latitude:Optional(-9.0) longitude:Optional(-3.0), stars: 4
Hotel latitude:Optional(-5.0) longitude:Optional(19.0), stars: 4
Hotel latitude:Optional(-9.0) longitude:Optional(-41.0), stars: 4
Hotel latitude:Optional(-19.0) longitude:Optional(-2.0), stars: 4
Hotel latitude:Optional(-23.0) longitude:Optional(33.0), stars: 4
Hotel latitude:Optional(-31.0) longitude:Optional(29.0), stars: 4
Hotel latitude:Optional(-22.0) longitude:Optional(-18.0), stars: 4
Hotel latitude:Optional(7.0) longitude:Optional(11.0), stars: 4
Hotel latitude:Optional(-28.0) longitude:Optional(21.0), stars: 4
Hotel latitude:Optional(-33.0) longitude:Optional(0.0), stars: 4
```

All Output ◇

# Implementation of the facade

Based on the sequence diagram and method of the service consumed by the client, the facade called `ServiceFindHotelNearBy` in our sample project will have the following code:

```
import Foundation

class ServiceFindHotelNearBy: ServiceFindHotelNearByProtocol {

    //return a list of hotel that corresponds to our criteria
    func findHotel(from: String, distanceMax: Double, stars: Int) ->
    [Hotel]? {
        let svcGeocoding = Geocoding()
        let svcFindPoi = FindPoi()
        let systemhotelCatalog = HotelCatalog()

        //Geocode our adress to GPS Points
        let fromLocation = svcGeocoding.getGeocoordinates(from)

        //retrieve all hotels in the catalog
        let allHotels = systemhotelCatalog.getCatalog()

        //find POI that corresponds to our criteria
        let results = svcFindPoi.findPoiNearBy(fromLocation,
        distanceMax: distanceMax, stars: stars, catalog: allHotels)
      return results
    }
}
```

The facade is well-described as follows:

- First, we make a connection to all the needed systems: the `Geocoding`, `FindPoi`, and `SystemHotelCatalog` Webservices (our subsystems).
- Then, we orchestrate our calls based on the sequence diagram.
- We first geocode the address into a GPS point.
- Then, we get `allHotels` from the `systemHotelCatalog` object (which represent a subsystem) because we need to send it as an argument to the `FindPoi` service.
- This is what we need to do in our next statement. We need to pass the `distanceMax` value, number of stars value, and GPS point we just geocoded as arguments of the `findPoiNearBy` method of the `FindPoi` service.
- Then, we return the results to the client.

As you can see, the facade has encapsulated all the needed calls to the subsystem, hiding the complexity of retrieving hotels corresponding to the wishes of the client. This concludes the description of the facade pattern.

# Summary

This chapter concludes the discovery of the seven structural patterns. The adapter pattern has much more in common with the bridge pattern. The main difference is in the purpose of the pattern.

A bridge separates an interface and its implementation, whereas an adapter changes the interface of an existing object.

The decorator adds a functionality to an object without changing its interface and should be transparent to the application. For the adapter, this is not the case, it is not transparent from the client perspective: the adapter is the named implementation of the interface that a client sees, so the adapter is not hidden from the client.

The proxy pattern doesn't change any interface. It defines substitute objects for other objects.

The facade pattern transforms high-level requests into low-level requests by communicating with other subsystems. It hides the complexity of these subsystems by providing a simple interface that the client can see.

In the next chapter, we will start with our first three behavioral patterns: the `Strategy,` `State,` and `Template` methods.

# 5
# Behavioral Patterns – Strategy, State, and Template Method

I hope you're still with us; now, we will introduce you to the third and last category of the design patterns, which is categorized as a **Gang of Four** (**GoF**) design patterns: the behavioral pattern. Behavioral patterns are dedicated to algorithms and communication between them.

As algorithms consist of several operations that are divided into different classes, behavioral patterns can handle the organization of such classes and the ways in which they can communicate with one another.

The behavioral category contains 11 patterns that we will discuss through four chapters. In this chapter, we will discuss the following three patterns:

- The strategy pattern
- The state pattern
- The template method pattern

## The strategy pattern
When you need to change part of an object's algorithm at runtime, without modifying the client, the strategy pattern is the appropriate pattern to be used.

It removes an algorithm from its host class and moves it to a separate class. The algorithm part that can change is the **strategy**. Every strategy uses the same interface. The class using the strategy pattern delegates the treatment of the algorithm to the strategy.

# Roles

The strategy pattern is used to create an interchangeable family of algorithms from which the required process is chosen at runtime.

The algorithm changes don't affect the client part. This pattern can be used in the following cases:

- The behavior of a class can be implemented by different algorithms where some of them are better in terms of execution time or memory consumption
- Choosing the appropriate algorithm with `if` conditions instruction complexify the code
- A system has similar classes where only the behavior changes; in this case, the strategy pattern allows you to group these classes in only one class, which greatly simplifies the interface for clients

# Design

The generic structure of the strategy platform is as follows:

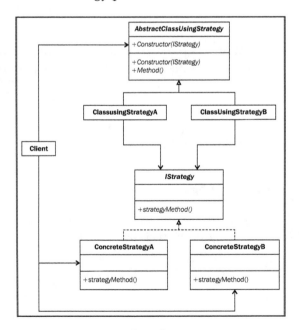

# Participants

The participants in the strategy pattern are as follows:

- IStrategy: This class defines the common interface implemented by all algorithms. This is the interface used by the ClassUsingStrategy class to invoke the right algorithm.

- ConcreteStrategyA and ConcreteStrategyB: These are concrete classes that implement different algorithms based on the IStrategy interface.

- ClassUsingStrategyA and ClassUsingStrategyB: These are classes that use an algorithm from classes that implement the IStrategy interface. These classes have a reference to one instance of one of the concrete strategy classes. These classes can expose some internal data to the implementation classes.

# Collaboration

The ClassUsingStrategy and ConcreteStrategy classes interact to implement algorithms.

In most cases, data needed by the algorithms is sent as arguments to the constructor but can be sent by a set property too. If needed, the ClassUsingStrategy class can provide you some methods to allow you to access its internal data.

The Client instance will initiate ClassUsingStrategy with a Strategy object and call the ClassUsingStrategy method that uses the strategy pattern.

Then, this class will send the request received from the client to the instance that is referenced by the strategy attribute.

# Illustration

We will see how to implement the strategy pattern using a simple example.

Some objects can move, but some of them don't move in the same manner. Each object has a particular manner in which it moves: some can walk and others can run and fly. The move behavior is our strategy, and we will encapsulate the performMove() action in the concrete strategy class that is referenced in the concrete class using the strategy.

# Implementation

Open the strategy pattern Xcode project to see the organization of our code. The participants in this pattern are separated in four folders, as shown in the following screenshot:

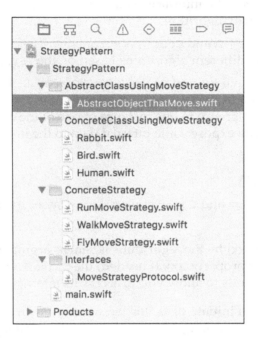

The first thing that we will do is define the interface of the move strategy and then describe AbstractClassUsingMoveStrategy.

The interface of the move strategy is really easy; we will only tell the class implementing the strategy that we are waiting for a performMove method.

The MoveStrategyProtocol.swift file is as follows:

```
//Common Interface used by algorithms
protocol MoveStrategyProtocol {
  func performMove()
}
```

Our abstract class needs to have a role to keep a reference to the strategy that will be applied by encapsulating the call to the performMove method of the current strategy into its own method that we will call move(). The instance of the strategy object will be received in the constructor of the class implementing the AbstractObjectThatMove class.

For our demo, we will add an internal computed property, WhoAmI, where we will set or get the name of the concrete class using the strategy pattern.

Our AbstractObjectThatMove.swift file is as follows:

```swift
class AbstractObjectThatMove {
  private var strategy: MoveStrategyProtocol!
  private var whoAmI:String = "Unknown Object"

  required init(strategy: MoveStrategyProtocol) {
    self.strategy = strategy
  }

  func move(){
    strategy.performMove()
  }

  internal var WhoAmi: String {
    get {
      return whoAmI
    }
    set {
      whoAmI = newValue
    }
  }
}
```

 Swift 2.0 has no support for abstract classes as yet. Here, we named the AbstractObjectThatMove class, even if it is not a "real" abstract class, only to be as close as possible to the general concept of the pattern. Nevertheless, there might be a way to have something that seems like an abstract class, but it differs from the general concept of the pattern where we pass a strategy to the initializer. Swift 2.0 has protocol extensions that give the opportunity to add partial implemented methods to protocols, and in "some way", make an abstract class:

```swift
protocol AbstractObjectThatMove {
    var WhoAmi: String { get set}
}
extension AbstractObjectThatMove {
    func move(strategy: IMoveStrategy) {
        strategy.performMove()
    }
}
```

```
class Human : AbstractObjectThatMove {
    var WhoAmi: String = "i'm a human"
}
```

Then, we can process the following code:

```
print("- *** working with Human")
let strategyForHuman = WalkMoveStrategy()
let human = Human()

// Tell who am I
print(human.WhoAmi)

//perform human move:
human.move(strategyForHuman)
```

So, we come back to the implementation of the pattern. In our current example, we have three concrete classes that implement the abstract classes: `Rabbit`, `Bird`, and `Human`. As the implementation is the same for all these three objects, I will only display the implementation of the concrete `Human` class:

```
class Human: AbstractObjectThatMove {
    required init(strategy: MoveStrategyProtocol){
        super.init(strategy: strategy)
        self.WhoAmi = "i'm a human"
    }
}
```

We want to add a value to the `WhoAmI` property while it is initializing, so we inform the `init` method that this method is required. We then set the value of the property with a simple `self.WhoAmi = "I'm a human"` statement.

> We could have done this by adding an additional parameter to the constructor defined in the `AbstractClass` that takes the value of WhoAmI and assigns it to the internal whoAmI variable too.

Now, we will implement `WalkMoveStrategy`, as defined in the `MoveStrategyProtocol` protocol:

```
class WalkMoveStrategy: MoveStrategyProtocol {
    func performMove() {
        print("I am walking")
    }
}
```

There's nothing complex here; we implement the `performMove` method and print the message of the move action. The `RunMoveStrategy` and `FlyMoveStrategy` methods are implemented in the same way; just the `print` statement changes:

```
Last, to complete the example, we will make our human, bird, and
   rabbit perform a move according to the strategy they
   apply:print("- *** working with Human")
let strategyForHuman = WalkMoveStrategy()
let human = Human(strategy: strategyForHuman)

// Tell who am I
print(human.WhoAmi)

//perform human move:
human.move()


print("- *** working with Bird")
let strategyForBid = FlyMoveStrategy()
let bird = Bird(strategy: strategyForBid)

// Tell who am I
print(bird.WhoAmi)

//perform human move:
bird.move()

print("- *** working with Rabbit")
let strategyForRabbit = RunMoveStrategy()
let rabbit = Rabbit(strategy: strategyForRabbit)

// Tell who am I
print(rabbit.WhoAmi)

//perform human move:
rabbit.move()
```

In the preceding highlighted code, you can see how we proceeded to apply the strategy to the `Human` class using the following steps:

1. First, we instantiate a strategy.

2. Next, we instantiate a concrete class using the strategy pattern where the strategy declared first is sent as an argument.

3. Then, we perform a move action in the concrete class. The move action invokes the `performMove` method of the strategy that the concrete class has in reference.

4. Click on the **Run** button to see the result.

You should see the following result in the console of Xcode:

```
- *** working with Human
i'm a human
I am walking
- *** working with Bird
i'm a bird
I am flying
- *** working with Rabbit
i'm a rabbit
I am running
Program ended with exit code: 0

All Output ◇                              🗑  □□
```

# The state pattern

In the state pattern, a class behavior changes based on its state. This type of design pattern comes under the behavior pattern.

In the state pattern, we create objects that represent various states and a context object whose behavior varies as its state object changes.

## Role

The role of this pattern is to adapt its behavior depending on the internal state of an object. It can be used when implementing the dependency of the state object if the condition statement becomes complex.

## Design

The generic class diagram structure of the state pattern is as follows:

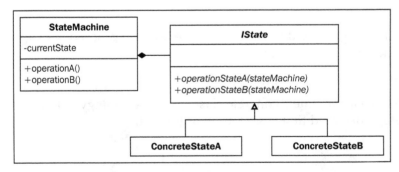

# Participants

The participants in the state pattern are as follows:

- `StateMachine`: This is a concrete class that describes a state machine's objects, which means that they have a set of states that can be described in a state transition diagram. This class has a reference to an instance of a sub class that implements the state abstract class and defines the current state.

- `IState`: This is an abstract class that introduces you to the methods signature of a state behavior.

- `ConcreteStateA` and `ConcreteStateB`: These are concrete subclasses that implement the behavioral methods depending on the state.

# Collaboration

The `StateMachine` object delegates the call of the method to a `ConcreteState` object depending on the current state.

The `StateMachine` object can send a reference to itself and to the `ConcreteState` object if needed. This reference can then be sent through the initialization of the `concreteState` object or each time calls are delegated.

# Illustration

Your company needs to sell a new device that has only two buttons that can play the radio or some music. You need to have the following functionalities, depending on the current state of the device:

| State | Action button | Source button |
|---|---|---|
| Radio | This changes to the next station and plays it | This changes to music playing mode |
| Playing music | This pauses the music | This changes to standby mode |
| Pausing music | This plays the music | This changes to standby mode |
| Standby | This changes to radio mode | This does nothing |

The preceding table shows us that we have four states to implement. Depending on the state, the button's behaviors will not be the same.

# Implementation

First, open the `StatePattern.xcodeproj` file to see the structure of the project.

Our audio player device is represented by the `Player.swift` class in the `ConcreteClassWithState` folder.

Our common interface that defines the method signature of a state behavior is defined in the `IPlayerState.swift` file. Each state that implements the `IPlayerState` interfaces are grouped in the `ConcreteState` folder.

The `main.swift` file contains our demo client:

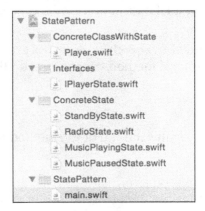

As always, we will first define our interface. Each state will implement a behavior for each of the two buttons visible on our audio player and pass the device object as an argument. This will allow the current state object to manipulate the current state of the audio player object:

```
protocol IAudioPlayerState{
    func buttonAction(player:AudioPlayer)
    func buttonSource(player:AudioPlayer)
}
```

Then, we can implement our audio player. The `init` method is waiting to receive a `concreteState` instance that we will keep in mind in the state variable.

We define our two buttons. Each of them will delegate the request to the state object by invoking the appropriate button.

We then add a computed property called `CurrentState` that allows us to return the current state of the audio player or to change it through the state objects.

The final code of the `AudioPlayer` class is as follows:

```
import Foundation

class AudioPlayer {
```

```
private var state:IAudioPlayerState!

required init(state:IAudioPlayerState){
  self.state = state
}

//Press the Action Button
func ActionButton(){
  state.buttonAction(self)
}

//Press the Source Button
func SourceButton(){
  state.buttonSource(self)
}

var CurrentState:IAudioPlayerState{
  get{
    return state
  }
  set{
    state = newValue
  }
}
}
```

Our player is now ready and the interface implemented by the state's objects is defined. We can now start with coding our first state: the RadioState class.

This class represents the state where the audio player plays the radio:

```
import Foundation

class RadioState: IAudioPlayerState {

  init(){
    print("RADIO MODE")
  }

  func buttonSource(player: AudioPlayer) {
    print("Changing to MUSIC Mode")
    player.CurrentState = MusicPlayingState()
  }

  func buttonAction(player: AudioPlayer) {
```

```
      print("Choosing next Station & playing it")
    }
  }
```

The implementation is quite simple; we inform the init() method that we are in the radio mode. We implement the IAudioPlayerState protocol and the buttonSource and buttonAction methods.

As we are in the radio mode, pressing buttonAction will change it to the next station, and clicking on the source button will move it to the MusicPlaying state.

To change the state of the audio player, we only need to make a call to the CurrentState property of the player object:

```
      player.CurrentState = MusicPlayingState()
```

Using the same logical implementation and based on the table in the preceding example, we can complete our code. The following code is the implementation of the MusicPlayingState class:

```
  class MusicPlayingState: IAudioPlayerState {

    init(){
      print("MUSIC PLAY MODE")
    }

    func buttonSource(player: AudioPlayer) {
      print("Changing source to Standby Mode")
      player.CurrentState = StandByState()
    }

    func buttonAction(player: AudioPlayer) {
      print("Changing to Pausing Mode")
      player.CurrentState = MusicPausedState()
    }
  }
```

The following code is the implementation of the MusicPausedState class:

```
  class MusicPausedState: IAudioPlayerState {

    init(){
      print("MUSIC PAUSED MODE")
    }

    func buttonSource(player: AudioPlayer) {
```

```
        print("Changing source to Standby Mode")
        player.CurrentState = StandByState()
    }

    func buttonAction(player: AudioPlayer) {
        print("Changing to playing Mode")
        player.CurrentState = MusicPlayingState()
    }
}
```

The following code is the implementation of the StandBySTate class:

```
class StandByState: IAudioPlayerState {

    init(){
        print("STANDBY MODE")
    }

    func buttonSource(player: AudioPlayer) {
        print("Changing to Radio Mode")
        player.CurrentState = RadioState()
    }

    func buttonAction(player: AudioPlayer) {
        print("cannot launch an action in standby mode")
    }
}
```

Our player is now ready to work. We will code our demo case to test whether the functionalities implemented are working as described in the table given in the introduction of the sample.

Open the main.swift file and write the following code:

```
let standbyMode = StandByState()
let player = AudioPlayer(state: standbyMode)

player.ActionButton()
player.SourceButton()

player.ActionButton()
player.SourceButton()

player.ActionButton()
player.ActionButton()
player.SourceButton()
```

First, we instantiate the first state where our audio player will be. We decide to put it in the StandBy mode.

Then, we instantiate our audio player and pass the standbymode state as an argument. Finally, we will simulate an action on by clicking the action or source button. Let's run the code, and you will see the result, as shown in the following example:

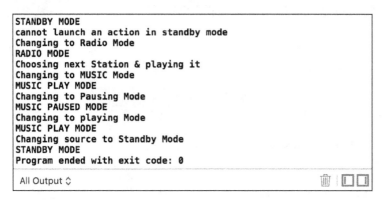

```
STANDBY MODE
cannot launch an action in standby mode
Changing to Radio Mode
RADIO MODE
Choosing next Station & playing it
Changing to MUSIC Mode
MUSIC PLAY MODE
Changing to Pausing Mode
MUSIC PAUSED MODE
Changing to playing Mode
MUSIC PLAY MODE
Changing source to Standby Mode
STANDBY MODE
Program ended with exit code: 0
```
All Output ◊

We start in the standby mode. The action button tells us that we cannot use it in the standby mode. So, we click on the source button and enter in the radioMode. We push the action button again; this changes to the next station and plays it.

We push the source button again and change to the music mode by playing the music. We push the action button and the music is paused. We then push the action button again and the music is played again.

Finally, we push the source button and the audio player comes back in the audio mode.

# The template method

The template method pattern is a simple pattern used when you need a general behavior but where the details of the algorithm must be specific to subclasses.

# Role

The template method pattern isolates various parts of an algorithm. The algorithm skeleton is defined in an abstract class where some steps of the algorithm are delegated to its subclasses and some others are fixed in the abstract class itself and cannot be overridden in subclasses.

# Design

The following diagram describes the generic structure of the template method:

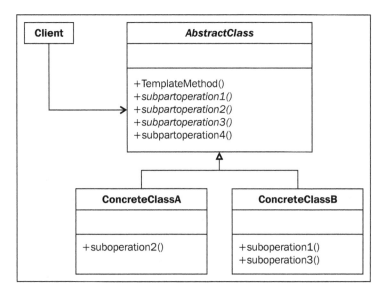

# Participants

The participants of this pattern are as follows:

- The AbstractClass, which defines the template method, and the signature of the sub parts of the algorithm are invoked by the template method.
- The ConcreteClass implements abstract methods used by the template method of the AbstractClass. It is possible to have several concrete classes.

# Collaboration

The algorithm defined in the template method is called TemplateMethod() in the generic UML class diagram and invokes parts of the algorithm in the subclasses.

# Illustration

You are working on a new simulation game with several personage types. Each personage has several properties, such as money, happiness, fatigue, hungry, and knowledge.

Each of these personages can "Play" a day. A day is decomposed in several parts:

- `GetUp`
- `EatBreakFast`
- `DoWashingUp`
- `GoToWork`
- `Work`
- `GoHome`
- `DoPersonalActivites`
- `EatDinner`
- `Sleep`

We have three types of personages: `Student`, `Searcher`, and `FireMan`; each of them can "play" a day but doesn't react in the same way depending on the day phase.

So, we will override parts of the algorithm in the concrete class by defining the personage type. The only part of the algorithm that is fixed is the `DoWashingUp` function. This part will not and cannot be overridden in subclasses.

# Implementation

Open the **TemplateMethod** project with Xcode. The project is quite simple. We will find the `TemplateMethod` folder in the `AbstractPersonage.Swift` class and all concrete subclasses that implement parts of the algorithm in the three concrete classes: `Searcher`, `Student`, and `FireMan`:

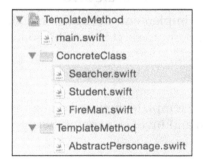

To implement the preceding example, we will first prepare our abstract class that defines a personage. Remember to consider this class as an abstract class. You must not instantiate it directly to your code, but you must instantiate only a subclass of AbstractPersonage:

```
class AbstractPersonage {
  private final var fatigue = 100
  private final var money = 0
  private final var happiness = 100
  private final var hungry = 100
  private final var knowledge = 100
  private final var name:String!

  final var canBePaid: Bool = true

  required init(name: String) {
   self.name = name
  }


  func toString() {
    print("("Name: \(name) / fatigue : \(Fatigue) / happiness
    \(Happiness) / Hungry \(Hungry) / knowledge \(Fatigue) /
    money: \(Money) / ")
  }

  //Play a day for the Personage
  func playDay() {
    print("PLAYING DAY")
    print("Get Up!")
    getUp()
    print("Eat Breakfast")
    eatBreakfast()
    doWashingUp()
    print("Go to work")
    goToWork()
    print("Work")
    work()

    if canBePaid {
      print("Receive Pay")
      getPaid()
```

```
  }
  print("BackHome")
  backToHome()

  print("Do personal activities")
  doPersonalActivities()

  print("Eat dinner")
  eatDinner()

  print("Sleep")
  sleep()
}


func getUp() {
  Fatigue = 0
  Happiness = 25
  Hungry = -25
  Knowledge = 0
}

func eatBreakfast() {
  Fatigue = -5
  Happiness = 25
  Hungry = 60
  Knowledge = 0
}
final func doWashingUp() {
  print("do washing up")
}

func goToWork() {
  Fatigue = -15
  Happiness = -15
  Hungry = -10
  Knowledge = 0
}
func work(){
  Fatigue = -40
  Happiness = -25
```

```
    Hungry = -40
    Knowledge = 25
}

func getPaid() {
  Money = 1000
}

func backHome() {
  Fatigue = -15
  Happiness = 10
  Hungry = -10
  Knowledge = 0
}

func doPersonalActivities() {
  Fatigue = -15
  Happiness = 15
  Hungry = -10
  Knowledge = 0
}

func eatDinner() {
  Fatigue = -10
  Happiness = 5
  Hungry = 40
  Knowledge = 0
}
func sleep() {
  Fatigue = 90
  Happiness = 0
  Hungry = -5
  Knowledge = 2
}

var Fatigue: Int {
  get{
    return fatigue
  }
  set{
```

```
      fatigue += newValue
      }
  }

  var Hungry: Int {
    get{
      return hungry
    }
    set{
      hungry += newValue
    }
  }

  var Happiness: Int {
    get{
      return happiness
    }
    set{
      happiness += newValue
    }
  }

  var Money: Int {
    get{
      return money
    }
    set{
      money += newValue
    }
  }

  var Knowledge: Int {
    get{
      return knowledge
    }
    set{
      knowledge += newValue
    }
  }
}
```

In the preceding code, we can distinguish three parts. The first part is a private variable declaration. We mark the access modifier to avoid modification in subclasses:

```
private final var fatigue = 100
private final var money = 0
...
```

Our playDay template method invokes all the parts of the algorithm:

```
//Play a day for the Personage
func playDay() {
  print("PLAYING DAY")
  print("Get Up!")
  getUp()
  print("Eat Breakfast")
  eatBreakfast()
  doWashingUp()
  print("Go to work")
  goToWork()
  print("Work")
  work()

  if canBePaid {
    print("Receive Pay")
    getPaid()
  }
  print("BackHome")
  backHome()

  print("Do personal activities")
  doPersonalActivities()

  print("Eat dinner")
  eatDinner()

 doWashingUp()

  print("Sleep")
  sleep()
}

...
```

Then, we define the method signatures that are parts of the algorithm and we will eventually implement them. Here, we define a default implementation of each method:

```
func eatBreakfast() {
    Fatigue = -5
    Happiness = 25
    Hungry = 60
    Knowledge = 0
}

func goToWork() {
    Fatigue = -15
    Happiness = -15
    Hungry = -10
    Knowledge = 0
}

//others methods
```

Finally, we define our computed properties to modify the setter behavior by making an addition to itself when a new value is assigned to the property:

```
var Fatigue: Int {
  get{
    return fatigue
  }
  set{
  fatigue += newValue
  }
}

var Hungry: Int {
  get{
    return hungry
  }
  set{
    hungry += newValue
  }
}
```

The following two steps make our sample better:

- We add a required constructor where we inject a name to the personage that we will instantiate:

```
required init(name: String) {
self.name = name
}
```

- We define a `toString()` method that will print all the properties and values of the personage:

```
func toString() {
   print("Name: \(name) / fatigue : \(Fatigue) / happiness
   \(Happiness) / Hungry \(Hungry) / knowledge \(Fatigue)
   / money: \(Money) / ")
}
```

Well, our abstract class that implements the template method is complete. Now, we have a skeleton to make a new concrete personage, for example, a student.

The student doesn't have a job, so he won't get paid. The student reads books during his personal activities.

So, we will create a new `Student` class that implements our abstract class that contains the template method, and we will override only parts of the algorithm that changes in the parent class:

```
class Student: AbstractPersonage {

   required init(name: String) {
     super.init(name: name)
     //student cannot be paid
     canBePaid = false
   }

   override func doPersonalActivities() {
     //student Read Books during its personal activities
     //so life indicators must be updated
     Fatigue = -5
     Happiness = 15
     Hungry = -5
     Knowledge = 15
   }
}
```

In the same way, we define the `Searcher` and `FireMan` classes that implement our abstract classes and both can be paid but not the same amount. Also, each of them must override some parts of the algorithm to be more accurate with specificity of the entity that the class represent:

For the `Searcher` class, we will implement the `AbstractPersonage` protocol as follows:

```
class Searcher: AbstractPersonage {

  override func getPaid() {
    Money = 3000/30
  }

  override func sleep() {
    //Searcher sleep very well
    Fatigue = 90
    Happiness = 0
    Hungry = -5
    Knowledge = 10
  }

  override func doPersonalActivitie() {
    //Searcher Read ScientificBooks during its personal activities
    //so life indicators must be updated
    Fatigue = -5
    Happiness = 10
    Hungry = -5
    Knowledge = 25
  }
}
```

For the `FireMan` class, we will implement it as follows:

```
import Foundation

class FireMan: AbstractPersonage {

  override func getPaid() {
    Money = 2500/30
  }

  override func sleep() {
    //FireMan doesn't sleep a lot
```

```
        Fatigue = 80
        Happiness = 5
        Hungry = -5
        Knowledge = 0
    }

    override func doPersonalActivities() {
        //FireMan makes lot of sports during personal activities
        //so life indicators must be updated
        Fatigue = -10
        Happiness = 5
        Hungry = -5
        Knowledge = 15
    }

    override func work() {
        Fatigue = -25
        Happiness = -55
        Hungry = -45
        Knowledge = 10
    }



}
```

Our template method and concrete classes are now ready. We can now write in the main.swift file. Our simple client will instantiate a student called Simon, a searcher called Natasha, and a fireman called Edward.

We will display the properties of each of them before simulating 30 days of their life. Then, we will tell these three personages to live for 30 days using the following code:

```
student.toString()
searcher.toString()
fireMan.toString()
```

Then, we will play 30 days of life in a for loop:

```
for i in 1...30{
    student.playDay()
    searcher.playDay()
    fireMan.playDay()
}
```

At the end of these 30 days of life, we will check the properties of each of them:

```
print("- **** 30 days later:")
student.toString()
searcher.toString()
fireMan.toString()
```

The final code is as follows:

```
import Foundation

let student = Student(name: "Simon")
let searcher = Searcher(name: "Natasha")
let fireMan = FireMan(name:"Edward")

print("- **** Starting with:")
student.toString()
searcher.toString()
fireMan.toString()

//Play a month
for i in 1...30{
  print("**************")
  print("Play Day \(i) ")
  print("**************")
  student.playDay()
  searcher.playDay()
  fireMan.playDay()
}
print("- **** 30 days later:")
student.toString()
searcher.toString()
fireMan.toString()
```

Click on the **Run** button. On the console, you will see the results after 30 days of life:

```
PLAYING DAY
Get Up!
Eat Breakfast
do washing up
Go to work
Work
Receive Pay
BackHome
Do personal activities
Eat dinner
do washing up
Sleep
- **** 30 days later:
Name: Simon / fatigue : 100 / happiness 1300 / Hungry 250 / knowledge 100 / money: 0 / |
Name: Natasha / fatigue : 100 / happiness 1150 / Hungry 250 / knowledge 100 / money: 3000 /
Name: Edward / fatigue : 100 / happiness 250 / Hungry 100 / knowledge 100 / money: 2490 /

All Output ◇
```

# Summary

There are similarities between the strategy and state patterns, but the main difference is one of intents:

- The strategy object encapsulates an algorithm
- The state object encapsulates a behavior that depends on the internal state of an object

In both the patterns, we use polymorphism. So, for both the patterns, we define a parent interface or abstract class, and then we implement the methods defined in the parent interface or abstract class in concrete subclasses. The pattern maintains the context and depending on it decides the appropriate object to use. The biggest difference between these two patterns is that we encapsulate an algorithm into strategy classes in the strategy pattern, but we encapsulate a state into state classes in the state pattern.

The template method pattern is more like the strategy pattern; it is based on the right application of an algorithm. In this pattern, all steps are specified in the template method and some subparts are deferred to subclasses.

In the next chapter, we will learn how to use two other behavioral patterns: chain of responsibility and command.

Both are used to pass requests for actions to appropriate objects.

# 6
# Behavioral Patterns – Chain of Responsibility and Command

In this chapter, we will continue to explore the behavioral patterns — the **chain of responsibility** and **command** patterns. Both of these patterns are concerned with passing requests to appropriate objects that will then execute the action.

The main difference between these two patterns is the way that the requests are passed between objects.

In this chapter, we will discuss the following topics:

- The chain of responsibility pattern
- The command pattern

## The chain of responsibility pattern

When you write an application, it may be that an event generated by an object needs to be handled by another object. You may also want the handle to be inaccessible by another object.

## Roles

In this section, you will notice that the chain of responsibility pattern creates a chain of objects in such a way that if an object of this chain cannot handle the request, it sends the request to the next object, the successor, until one of them can handle the request.

This pattern allows an object to send a request without knowing which object will receive and handle it. The request is sent from one object to another, making them parts of a chain. Each object of this chain can handle the request, pass it to its successor, or do both.

You may want to use this pattern when:

- You want to decouple the sender of a request to its receiver, allowing other objects to handle the request too

- Objects that can handle the request are part of a chain of work, the request passes from one object to another until at least one of these objects can handle it

- You want to allow objects that can process requests to be ordered in a preferential sequence that can be reordered, without having any impact on the calling component

# Design

The following diagram illustrates the generic representation of the chain of responsibility pattern:

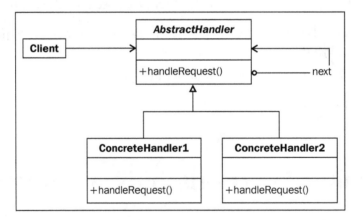

# Participants

This pattern has three participants, which are as follows:

- `AbstractHandler`: This defines the interface of the requests and implements the association of the chain of responsibility pattern.

- ConcreteHandlers: These objects can handle requests that they are responsible for. If it cannot handle the request, it passes the request to its successor or stops the chain.

- Client: The client sends the request to the first object of the chain that may handle the request.

# Collaboration

The following sequence diagram illustrates the collaboration between objects:

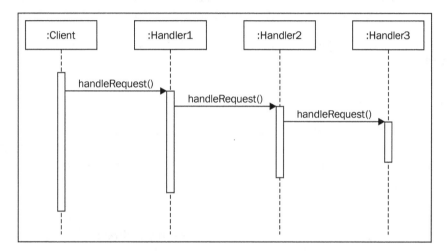

The client sends the request to the first object of the chain. Then, this request is propagated throughout the chain until at least one of the objects of the chain can handle it.

# Illustration

Suppose that you are supervising the development of a mobile application, and you want to handle some log messages differently, depending on the priority of the logger.

You define three types of priority, which means three levels of loggers: DEBUG, INFO, and ERROR.

Depending on the level of the log messages, you can handle it as follows:

- If the level (or priority) is DEBUG, then this will be handled by the standard output logger
- If the level is INFO, then we will use the standard output logger and e-mail logger that will send an e-mail with the message
- If the level is ERROR, then all the three loggers will handle the message: the standard output logger, e-mail logger, and error logger

As we can see here, we need to define a chain of objects in the following order: StdOutLogger, EmailLogger, and ErrorLogger.

The client will then only call the first concrete handler, the class that may handle the request: StdOutLogger.

# Implementation

To implement our pattern, we will need to prepare our abstract class first. Remember that with Swift, an abstract class does not really exist. We will write our abstract class as a class, but methods that need to be overridden will have the following statement:

```
preconditionFailure("Must be overridden")
```

In this case, if the code of the abstract class is called instead of the one available in the derived class, an exception similar to the following will be raised:

```
Building the Chain
fatal error: Must be overriden: file /Users/Admin/
Dropbox/Documents/Ebooks reviews/Ecriture Swift Design
Patterns/chapitres/Chapter6/code/CORPattern/
ChainOfResponsibilityPattern/
ChainOfResponsibilityPattern/Logger.swift, line 34
Program ended with exit code: 9
```

Let's now begin with the implementation.

First, open the ChainOfResponsibilityPattern project that you will find in the Chapter 6 folder.

The project is organized with the following structure:

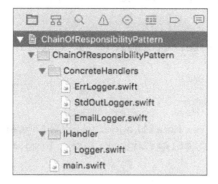

There's nothing complex here; we will define our chain and make a call to the main.swift file. The abstract class is defined in the Logger.swift file, and our three concreteHandlers classes have their own respective Swift files.

We will define the abstract class as follows:

```swift
class Logger {
    static var ERROR = 1
    static var INFO = 2
    static var DEBUG = 3

    var mask:Int?
    var next:Logger?

    func nextHandler(nextLogger:Logger) -> Logger? {
      next = nextLogger
      return next
    }

    func message(message: String, priority: Int){
      if priority <= mask {
        writeMessage(message)
        if let next = next {
          next.message(message, priority: priority)
        }
      }
    }
}
```

```
func writeMessage(message: String) {
  preconditionFailure("Must be overridden")
}

static func prepareDefaultChain() -> Logger? {
  var l: Logger?
  var ll: Logger?

  l = StdOutLogger(mask: Logger.DEBUG)
  ll = l!.nextHandler(EmailLogger(mask: Logger.INFO))
  ll = ll!.nextHandler(ErrLogger(mask: Logger.ERROR))
  return l
}}
```

We define three static variables that will represent our different levels of logs: ERROR, INFO, and DEBUG.

Then, we have two other variables that are declared, which are as follows:

- **Mask**: This variable is intrinsic to the object and will be set during the initialization of the handler. This variable will be used to compare its value against the level of the received request, which means that if the mask is less than or equal to the level, the object will be able to handle the request.

- **Next**: This variable is also intrinsic to the object and this permits the chaining. This variable contains the next ConcreteHandler where the request will be passed.

We have the following three functions:

- func nextHandler(...): This is a function that allows you to assign the next concrete handler to the next variable. Note that this function returns a logger. This is called nextLogger.

  So, if we write the following statement:

  ```
  l = StdOutLogger(mask: Logger.DEBUG)
  ll = l!.nextHandler(EmailLogger(mask: Logger.INFO))
  ```

  Then, ll is an EmailLogger instance and not a StdOutLogger.

- func message(...): This is the main function that has the responsibility (or not) to process the request and/or pass it to the next object of the chain.

- `writeMessage(...)`: This function is called by the `message(...)` function to simulate the work applied on the request. Here, we will only display a message that is linked to the current concrete handler object. Since we are in an abstract class, we add a `preconditionfailure(...)` statement that will inform us that `this` function must be overridden in the derived class. If the code is executed and the derived class does not override `this` method, a fatal error will be raised, which is explained in the *Implementation* section of this pattern.

- `prepareDefaultChain(...)`: This is a class function that encapsulates the creation of our default chain.

Our abstract class is now ready; we have only to write our derived classes. Remember that the `writeMessage(...)` function must be overridden, and we need to initialize the mask of our concrete handler.

First, let's take a look at the `StdOutLogger` concrete handler, which is as follows:

```
class StdOutLogger: Logger {
  init(mask: Int) {
    super.init()
    self.mask = mask
  }

  override func writeMessage(message: String) {
    print("Sending to StdOutLogger: \(message)")
  }
}
```

Next, we have the `EmailLogger` class:

```
class EmailLogger: Logger {
  init(mask: Int) {
    super.init()
    self.mask = mask
  }

  override func writeMessage(message: String) {
    print("Sending by Email: \(message)")
  }
}
```

In addition, we have the `ErrLogger` class:

```
class ErrLogger: Logger {
  init(mask: Int) {
    super.init()
    self.mask = mask
  }

  override func writeMessage(message: String) {
    print("Sending to ErrorLogger: \(message)")
  }
}
```

All of our concrete handlers are now ready. It is time for us to write our test in the `main.swift` file.

We first prepare our chain using the `Logger` class function, `prepareDefaultChain`:

```
print("Building the Chain")
var l: Logger?

l = Logger.prepareDefaultChain()
```

Then, we send a request (a string message with a logger type) to the first object of the chain (l is `StdOutLogger`):

```
print("- *** stdOutLogger:")
// Handled by StdOutLogger
l?.message("Entering the func Y()", priority: Logger.DEBUG)

print("- StdOutLogger && EmailLogger:")
// Handled by StdOutLogger && EmailLogger
l?.message("Step 1 Completed", priority: Logger.INFO)


print("- all three loggers:")
// Handled by all Logger
l?.message("An error occurred", priority: Logger.ERR)
```

Now, we will build and run the project. You will see the following result on the console:

```
Building the Chain
- *** stdOutLogger:
Sending to StdOutLogger: Entering the func Y()
- StdOutLogger && EmailLogger:
Sending to StdOutLogger: Step 1 Completed
Sending by Email: Step 1 Completed
- all three loggers:
Sending to StdOutLogger: An error occured
Sending by Email: An error occured
Sending to ErrorLogger: An error occured
Program ended with exit code: 0
```

The console output is very clear. The first handler has handled the first request only, and the second request has been handled by the StdOutLogger class and the EmailLogger class. The third request has been handled by all three handlers.

# The command pattern

The concept behind this pattern is to transform a request into an object in order to facilitate some actions, such as undo/redo, insertion into a queue, or tracking of the request.

# Roles

The command pattern creates distance between the client that requests an operation and the object that can perform it. The request is encapsulated into an object. This object contains a reference to the receiver who will effectively execute the operation.

The real operation is managed by the receiver and the command is like an order; it only contains a reference to the invoker, the object that will perform the action and an execute function will call the real operation on the worker.

This pattern allows the following features:

- Sending requests to different receivers
- Queuing, logging, and rejecting requests
- Undoable actions (the execute method can memorize the state and allows you to go back to that state)
- Encapsulate a request in an object
- Allows the parameterization of clients with different requests

# Design

The generic diagram class is represented as follows:

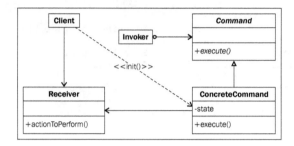

# Participants

The classes participating in this pattern are as follows:

- Command: This declares the interface for executing an operation.
- ConcreteCommand: This implements the Command interface with the execute method by invoking the corresponding operations on Receiver. It defines a link between the Receiver class and the action.
- Client: This creates a ConcreteCommand object and sets its receiver.
- Invoker: This asks the command to carry out the request.
- Receiver: This knows how to perform the operations.

# Collaboration

The following sequence diagram defines the collaboration between all objects participating in the command pattern:

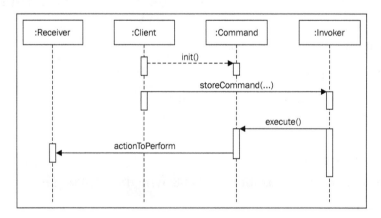

Let's discuss the preceding diagram in detail:

- The client asks for a command to be executed and specifies its receivers
- The client then sends the command to the invoker that stores it (or places it in a queue system if some actions needs to be performed before execution of the command) in order to execute it later
- The invoker is then called to launch the command by invoking the execute function on the appropriate command object
- The concrete command asks the receiver to execute the appropriate operation

# Illustration

Imagine that your company is working on a new universal controller that can manage up to four commands. This controller has four slots where we can add two commands to each of them. Near each slot, we have two buttons: the "On" and "Off" buttons.

Your team has already two objects and their specifications that allow a remote control to manipulate them:

- The objects that we will work with are a light and audio player
- The light can only be turned on and off
- The audio player can be turned on or off, and we can play or stop the music

Your job is to conceptualize commands that will be stored in the universal remote controller.

When we press the on or off button of a slot, the appropriate command should be sent to the appropriate device (the audio player or the light).

 In this example, we will not implement the undo/redo action. We will show you another pattern that is dedicated to this situation in the next chapter.

# Implementation

Open the Xcode project called `CommandPattern.xcodeproj`. Here is the organization of our project:

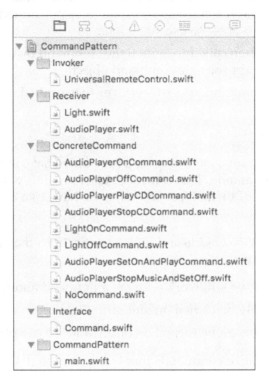

The structure of our project reflects the class diagram that we have seen in the *Design* section of the command pattern:

- We have the `Invoker` folder that contains our `UniversalRemoteController` object

- The `Receiver` folder contains two devices that will be able to receive commands to execute the appropriate operation

- The `Interface` folder contains the definition of a command

- The `ConcreteCommand` folder contains all the commands that we want to use with our universal remote controller

- Lastly, the `main.swift` file contains the code that will allow us to see the demo

To implement this example, let's begin with defining our `Command` interface.

We only need an `execute()` method to execute the command:

```
protocol ICommand {
  func execute()
}
```

Before we write our concrete command objects, let's see how our `Light` and `AudioPlayer` objects are implemented:

```
class Light {

  func on() {
    print("Light is On")
  }

  func off() {
    print("Light is Off")
  }
}
```

It is quite simple; the `on()` function will turn on the light and the `off()` function will turn it off.

Now, let's define the `AudioPlayer` class:

```
class AudioPlayer {

  enum AudioPlayerState {
    case On
    case Off
    case Playing
  }

  private var state = AudioPlayerState.Off

  func on() {
    state = AudioPlayerState.On
    print("Audio Player is On")
  }

  func off() {
    state = AudioPlayerState.Off
    print("Audio Player is Off")
  }
```

```
func playCD(){
  if state == AudioPlayerState.Off {
    print("doesn't work : the audio player is currently off")
  } else {
    state = AudioPlayerState.Playing
    print("AudioPlayer is playing")
  }
}

func stopCD(){
  if state == AudioPlayerState.Off {
    print("doesn't work : the audio player is currently off")
  }
  if state == AudioPlayerState.On {
    print("doesn't work : the audio player currently doesn't
    play music")
  } else {
    state = AudioPlayerState.On
    print("AudioPlayer has stopped to play music")
  }
}
}
```

This object is more complex. We have the same on() and off() methods, but we also have the playCD() and StopCD() methods.

We see that this object has an internal state. The state changes depending on the function called and the state is also used to control if the asked function is possible.

Now that we have all the necessary information, we can start writing our commands.

Let's begin with the light. What we want is to be able to use our universal remote controller to turn a light on or off, depending on the button pushed near the slot.

Therefore, we can first write our LightOnCommand concrete command object:

```
class LightOnCommand: ICommand {

  var light:Light

  init(light: Light) {
    self.light = light
  }
```

```
     func execute() {
        self.light.on()
     }
  }
```

Here, we created an object called `LightOnCommand` that implements the `ICommand` interface.

The command needs to know what the receiver object is, so we pass an argument to it during the initialization of the object:

```
  init(light: Light) {
     self.light = light
  }
```

Then, the `execute` method encapsulates the call to the `on()` function of the `Light` object to effectively process the command.

That's all; your `LightOnCommand` object is now ready.

We do the same with the `LightOffCommand` class and make changes wherever it is appropriate in order to use the `off()` function of the `Light` object instead of `on()`:

```
  class LightOffCommand: ICommand {

     var light:Light

     init(light: Light) {
        self.light = light
     }

     func execute() {
        self.light.off()
     }
  }
```

Our commands to control lights are both ready. Let's now see what we will do for the audio player. What we want is to be able to turn on or off the audio player, play, or stop music. These commands are similar to what we have already done with the light.

The `AudioPlayerOnCommand` class is written as follows:

```
class AudioPlayerOnCommand: ICommand {
  var audioPlayer:AudioPlayer

  init(audioPlayer:AudioPlayer) {
    self.audioPlayer = audioPlayer
  }

  func execute() {
    audioPlayer.on()
  }
}
```

The `AudioPlayerOffCommand` class is written as follows:

```
class AudioPlayerOffCommand: ICommand {
  var audioPlayer:AudioPlayer

  init(audioPlayer:AudioPlayer) {
    self.audioPlayer = audioPlayer
  }

  func execute() {
    audioPlayer.off()
  }
}
```

The `AudioPlayerPlayCdCommand` class is written as follows:

```
class AudioPlayerPlayCDCommand: ICommand {
  var audioPlayer:AudioPlayer

  init(audioPlayer:AudioPlayer) {
    self.audioPlayer = audioPlayer
  }

  func execute() {
    audioPlayer.playCD()
  }
}
```

The `AudioPlayerStopCDCommand` class is written as follows:

```
class AudioPlayerStopCDCommand: ICommand {
  var audioPlayer:AudioPlayer

  init(audioPlayer:AudioPlayer) {
    self.audioPlayer = audioPlayer
  }

  func execute() {
    audioPlayer.stopCD()
  }
}
```

At this point, all the commands needed are written.

We want to use our remote controller that has only four slots, as shown in the following diagram. With the remote controller, we want to be able to manipulate two lights: one in the bedroom, one in the hall, and an audio player to play and stop music:

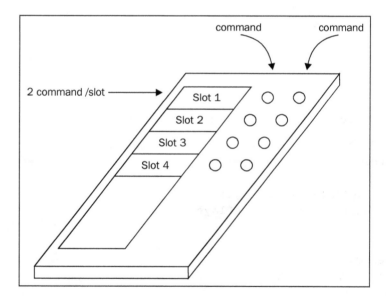

Why not create a command that will turn on the audio player and play the music in the same command object? Indeed, using our remote controller to execute only the on or off command is useless. What we want is to play or stop the music.

Imagine that you want to be able to turn on the audio player and play the CD only by pressing one button; in the same way, you want to be able to stop the CD player and turn off the audio player only by pressing one button.

To implement this, we only have to encapsulate appropriate functions of the audio player object on the execute function of the command. When our remote controller will invoke the execute method, we will first call the on function of the audioPlayer class and then the playCD() function:

```
class AudioPlayerSetOnAndPlayCommand: ICommand {
  var audioPlayer:AudioPlayer

  init(audioPlayer:AudioPlayer) {
    self.audioPlayer = audioPlayer
  }

  func execute() {
    audioPlayer.on()
    audioPlayer.playCD()
  }

}
```

Similarly, we proceed with our StopMusicAndSetOff command:

```
class AudioPlayerStopMusicAndSetOff: ICommand {
  var audioPlayer:AudioPlayer

  init(audioPlayer:AudioPlayer) {
    self.audioPlayer = audioPlayer
  }

  func execute() {
    audioPlayer.stopCD()
    audioPlayer.off()
  }

}
```

Our devices are ready to accept commands and command objects are ready. Before we start writing our demo code, let's see how the remote controller works:

```
class UniversalRemoteControl {
  var onCommands = [ICommand]()
  var offCommands = [ICommand]()

  init() {
    for _ in 1...4 {
      onCommands.append(NoCommand())
      offCommands.append(NoCommand())
    }
  }

  func addCommandToSlot(slot:Int, onCommand:ICommand,
  offCommand:ICommand) {
    onCommands[slot] = onCommand
    offCommands[slot] = offCommand
  }

  func buttonOnIsPushedOnSlot(slot:Int) {
    onCommands[slot].execute()
  }

  func buttonOffIsPushedOnSlot(slot:Int) {
    offCommands[slot].execute()
  }
}
```

When the remote controller is initialized, the four slots have a NoCommand object that is assigned. This object is as follows:

```
class NoCommand: ICommand {

  func execute() {
    print("No command associated to this")
  }
}
```

So, if we do not use the addCommandToSlot (...) function, each button will call the execute function of the NoCommand object, which means that there is nothing to do.

The remote controller has two buttons near each slot. Depending on the button and slot, buttonOnIsPushedOnSlot (...) or buttonOffIsPushedOnSlot is called.

As commands are stored in the `onCommands` and `offCommands` arrays, when `addCommandToSlot` is called, we call the `execute` command of the appropriate object. To execute the on command of a slot, we will run the following code:

```
onCommands[slot].execute()
```

To execute the off command of the same slot we will also run the following code:

```
offCommands[slot].execute()
```

Here, `slot` is the index of the button slot. Now, it is time to implement our demo code.

First, we initialize our remote controller, create our `audioPlayer`, and create our two lights: the bedroom light and hall light:

```
let uRemoteControl = UniversalRemoteControl()

let audioPlayerLivingRoom = AudioPlayer()
let lightBedroom = Light()
let lightHall = Light()
```

Then, we create all our command objects:

```
// MARK: Definition of our commands
let bedroomLightOnCommand = LightOnCommand(light: lightBedroom)
let bedroomLightOffCommand = LightOffCommand(light: lightBedroom)

let hallLightOnCommand = LightOnCommand(light: lightHall)
let hallLightOffCommand = LightOffCommand(light: lightHall)

let audioPlayerLivingRoomOnCommand =
  AudioPlayerOnCommand(audioPlayer: audioPlayerLivingRoom)
let audioPlayerLivingRoomOffCommand =
  AudioPlayerOffCommand(audioPlayer: audioPlayerLivingRoom)

let audioPlayerOnAndPlayLivingRoom =
  AudioPlayerSetOnAndPlayCommand(audioPlayer:
  audioPlayerLivingRoom)
let audioPlayerStopAndOffLivingRoom =
  AudioPlayerStopMusicAndSetOff(audioPlayer:
  audioPlayerLivingRoom)
```

Once our commands are ready, we can assign them to the remote controller using the addCommandToSlot function:

```
// Mark: Assign commands to the remote controller
uRemoteControl.addCommandToSlot(0, onCommand:
   bedroomLightOnCommand, offCommand: bedroomLightOffCommand)
uRemoteControl.addCommandToSlot(1, onCommand: hallLightOnCommand,
   offCommand: hallLightOffCommand)

uRemoteControl.addCommandToSlot(2, onCommand:
   audioPlayerLivingRoomOnCommand, offCommand:
   audioPlayerLivingRoomOffCommand)
uRemoteControl.addCommandToSlot(3, onCommand:
   audioPlayerOnAndPlayLivingRoom, offCommand:
   audioPlayerStopAndOffLivingRoom)
```

The last thing that is needed for the demo is to simulate the press on each button:

```
// Mark: Usage of the remote controller
uRemoteControl.buttonOnIsPushedOnSlot(0)
uRemoteControl.buttonOffIsPushedOnSlot(0)

uRemoteControl.buttonOnIsPushedOnSlot(1)
uRemoteControl.buttonOffIsPushedOnSlot(1)

uRemoteControl.buttonOnIsPushedOnSlot(2)
uRemoteControl.buttonOffIsPushedOnSlot(2)

uRemoteControl.buttonOnIsPushedOnSlot(3)
uRemoteControl.buttonOffIsPushedOnSlot(3)
```

Here, note that we have not added the concurrency protection. If the command is used by several components, we should make sure that the concurrency protection is added.

For this, we need to create a queue that will receive all the commands, execute them in a synchronous way, and have the first command receive in the queue, being the first command executed (first in first out). To see how to implement concurrency protection, you can check the implementation of the mediator pattern in *Chapter 7, Behavioral Patterns – Iterator, Mediator, and Observer* and the note about concurrency protection available in the same chapter.

Click on build and run the demo.

You will now see the following result on the console, corresponding to each button pressed on the universal remote controller:

```
Light is On
Light is Off
Light is On
Light is Off
Audio Player is On
Audio Player is Off
Audio Player is On
AudioPlayer is playing
AudioPlayer has stopped to play music
Audio Player is Off
```

# Comparison between the chain of responsibility and command patterns

The difference between the two patterns is the way in which the request is decoupled.

In the chain of responsibility pattern, the request is passed to potential receivers, whereas the command pattern uses a command object that encapsulates a request.

The following table describes the difference between the chain of responsibility and command patterns:

|  | Chain of responsibility | Command |
| --- | --- | --- |
| Client creates | Handler objects | Command objects |
| Different kinds of | Handler classes at different levels | Command classes and receiver classes |
| Client can work with | Multiple handlers | Different receivers |
| Client calls | Handler objects | Receiver objects |
| Work is done in | `HandleRequest` in a handler | `ActionToPerform` in a receiver |
| Decision based on | Mask in handlers | Routing in commands |

# Summary

I hope this chapter was interesting. In this chapter, we learned how to decouple senders and receivers in both the chain of responsibility and command patterns, thus improving the layering and reusability of a system.

In the next chapter, we will explore three new patterns: the iterator, mediator, and observer patterns that are dedicated to the communication between objects while maintaining their independence.

# 7
# Behavioral Patterns – Iterator, Mediator, and Observer

This chapter presents you with three other behavioral patterns, which support communication between objects. Objects keep their independence and sometimes their anonymity. The iterator pattern is often used with array, collection, and dictionary objects. The mediator allows communication between two objects without knowing each other's identities and the observer patterns mirror the publish/subscribe methodologies that are well known in distributed systems.

This chapter is divided in three sections:

- The iterator pattern
- The mediator pattern
- The observer pattern

## The iterator pattern

This pattern is commonly used in many languages with an array or a collection of objects. It allows iteration over a list of objects contained in a collection.

## Roles

The iterator pattern allows you to iterate sequentially over an aggregated object of objects without having to know how the collection is structured.

# Design

Here, you'll find the generic UML class diagram of the pattern, but note that we will not implement it using this way.

Indeed, Swift provides some types that will simplify the implementation of the iterator pattern, without having to produce all of the needed requirements by hand.

Why reinvent the wheel? The following figure represents the generic UML class diagram:

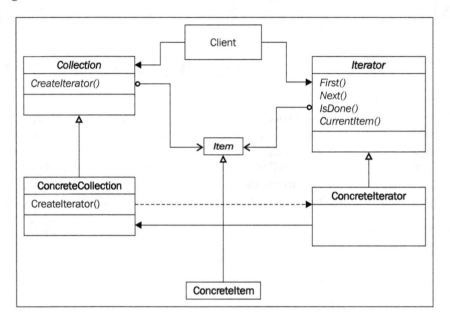

# Participants

As with every pattern described up to now, I will tell you what the participants in this pattern are even if we will not see all of them in our implementation of the pattern:

- `Collection`: This is an abstract class that implements the association of the collection with items and the `CreateIterator()` method

- `ConcreteCollection`: This is concrete collection subclass that link the `CurrentItem` object to a `ConcreteItem` object and the `Iterator` interface to the `ConcreteIterator` object

- `Iterator`: This is the abstract class, which implements the association of the iterator and the collection items and methods
- `ConcreteIterator`: This is a concrete subclass that links our `currentItem` to the `ConcreteItem` object
- `Item`: This is the abstract class of the collection items
- `ConcreteItem`: This is a concrete `Item` subclass used by `ConcreteIterator` and `ConcreteCollection`

# Collaboration

The iterator keeps in memory the current item in the collection. It can also calculate and predict the next object of the iteration.

# Illustration

You are developing a game in which you can have up to say, four players. You want to be able to iterate over all the four players to do something. In our sample, we will display the name of each player.

# Implementation

The implementation provided here comes from ideas discovered on the Lilly Labs website at `http://lillylabs.no/2014/09/30/make-iterable-swift-collection-type-sequencetype/`.

Well, given our illustration what we want to be able to do is to iterate using a `for...in` loop construct.

All thanks to Swift, we have some elements that will simplify the implementation of this pattern.

Indeed, Swift proposes a `SequenceType` protocol and an `AnyGeneratorType<T>` class, which implements the `GeneratorType` protocol.

The `SequenceType` protocol defines a protocol that allows us to iterate over elements of a collection using the `for...in` loop construct. It requires that the class implements the `generate()` method, which returns an object conforming to the `GeneratorType` protocol.

`AnyGenerator<T>` is a class that conforms to the `GeneratorType` protocol, where `<T>` means `Item` of any type.

Having said this, how do we use all of the preceding functions to easily iterate over a collection of any type? Let's say, we have the following class:

```
class Player {
  var name: String!

  init(name: String) {
   self.name = name
  }
}
```

Therefore, we define a simple `Player` class where we pass a string in the constructor, which corresponds to the name of the player.

We suppose that we have four players in our game and want to be able to iterate over each of them to display their name.

Therefore, the final code to test will be something like the following:

```
for player in players {
  print("analysing \(player.name)")
}
```

Now, how to complete our code with a bonus, something that will works with any class that we want to iterate over? Well, we will use another concept provided by Swift: **extension**.

The first thing to be done is to create an object or struct that we will let us iterate over any class type:

```
struct OurCollection<T> {
  let items: [T]
}
```

Therefore, we define a struct that we call `OurCollection`, where items are of type `T`.

Now, we will be able to write the following:

```
let player1 = Player(name: "Helmi")
let player2 = Player(name: "Raphael")
let player3 = Player(name: "Adrien")
let player4 = Player(name: "Alain")

let players = OurCollection(items:[player1,player2, player3,
  player4])
```

However, the `for...in` loop will still not work, as shown in the following screenshot:

```
45  for player in players {                    Type 'OurCollection<Player>' does not conform to protocol 'SequenceType'
46      print("analysing \(player.name)")
47  }
```

Even though, the players don't implement the `SequenceType` protocol. Here is the magic:

```
extension OurCollection: SequenceType {
  typealias Generator = AnyGenerator<T>

  func generate() -> Generator {
    var i = 0
    return anyGenerator {
      return i >= self.items.count ? nil : self.items[i++]
    }
  }
}
```

Wow! Lot of new things here:

First, we create an extension of the `OurCollection` struct by telling that we want to implement the `SequenceType` protocol.

So we implement the `generate()` method, which will return the next type `T` object in the iteration. Also, note the line:

```
func generate() -> Generator {
```

Generator is an alias of `AnyGenerator<T>`:

```
typealias Generator = AnyGenerator<T>
```

We use this to simplify the writing. We can remove the type alias statement and write:

```
func generate() -> AnyGenerator<T> {
```

Another function is the `anyGenerator` function tha you see here:

```
return anyGenerator {
  return i >= self.items.count ? nil : self.items[i++]
}
```

The Swift 2.0 documentation says that the `anyGenerator` function has the following signature:

```
func anyGenerator<Element>(body: () -> Element?) ->
  AnyGenerator<Element>
```

The purpose of this function is to return a `GeneratorType` instance whose `next` method invokes `body` and returns the result.

So here, we start from index 0 to index `self.items.count` value and add the `sel.items[i++]` in the new `GeneratorType` instance. The new `GeneratorType` instance is returned when `i` is superior to a number of elements in the items array.

We can also write the function such as:

```
func generate() -> Generator {
  var i = 0
  let seq = anyGenerator {i < self.items.count ? self.items[i++]
  : nil}
  return seq
}
```

And also like this:

```
func generate() -> Generator {
  var i = 0
  return anyGenerator {i < self.items.count ? self.items[i++] :
  nil}
}
```

Here, we use a closure with the `anyGenerator` function to return a new sequence of elements that we can iterate over. Our final code is as follows:

```
import Foundation

struct OurCollection<T> {
  let items: [T]
}

class Player {
  var name: String!

  init(name: String) {
   self.name = name
  }
}

extension OurCollection: SequenceType {
```

```
    typealias Generator = AnyGenerator<T>

    func generate() -> Generator{
      var i = 0
      // Construct a AnyGenerator<T> instance, passing a closure
      // that returns the next type T object in the iteration
      return anyGenerator {
        return i >= self.items.count ? nil : self.items[i++]
      }
    }
}


let player1 = Player(name: "Helmi")
let player2 = Player(name: "Raphael")
let player3 = Player(name: "Adrien")
let player4 = Player(name: "Alain")


let players = OurCollection(items:[player1,player2, player3,
  player4])

for player in players {
  print("Name: \(player.name)")
}
```

Open the `iteratorPattern` project, build and run it. You will now see the
following result:

```
Name: Helmi
Name: Raphael
Name: Adrien
Name: Alain
Program ended with exit code: 0
```

# The mediator pattern

The mediator pattern is used to reduce the coupling between classes that
communicate with each other.

# Roles

This pattern constructs an object, which manages the communication between two
or more classes.

These classes don't know each other's implementation. The message is sent from the class to the mediator object.

The mediator pattern defines an object that encapsulates how a set of objects will communicate with each other. Mediator promotes loose coupling by keeping objects from referring to each other explicitly and it also lets you vary their interaction independently.

The mediator is an intermediary used to decouple many peers. This pattern can be used when we want to design reusable components but dependencies between the potentially reusable pieces demonstrate the "spaghetti code" phenomenon.

# Design

The following class diagram presents the generic structure of the mediator pattern:

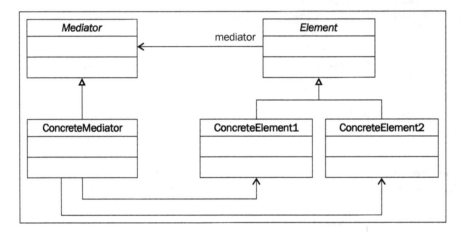

# Participants

In this pattern, we find the following participants:

- `Mediator`: This defines the mediator interface to communicate with elements
- `ConcreteMediator`: This implements the coordination between elements and manages associations with elements
- `Elements`: This is the element abstract class, which introduces common attributes, properties, and methods
- `ConcreteElement1` and `ConcreteElement2`: These are concretes element classes, which communicate with the mediator instead of communicating with the other elements

# Collaboration

The elements send messages to the mediator and receive message from it. The mediator implements the collaboration and coordination between the elements.

# Illustration

You are writing a system that allows users to communicate with each other. Communication is not sent directly from a peer to another. We will use some mediators that will manage all users and the communication between them.

For this, each user managed by the mediator will be registered (added) to the mediator. Then, when a user sends a message, we will pass the mediator object as an argument informing the system that this is the message that will broadcast that message to all other users managed by the mediator calling the receiveMessage function.

# Implementation

Open the MediatorPattern Xcode project. This is a command line project that is organized as the following screenshot:

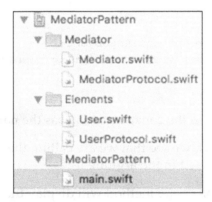

The organization of our project is not more than what we have already described with the participants in the class diagram. We retrieve, the MediatorProtocol and ConcreteMediator object in the Mediator folder, our Elements and concrete elements UserProtocol and User are in the Elements folder and last, the main. swift file contains our client code to simulate the project.

First, we define `userProtocol`, in the `UserProtocol.swift` file:

```
protocol UserProtocol {
   func sendMessage(mediator:MediatorProtocol, message:AnyObject)
   func receiveMessage(message:AnyObject)
}
```

The `sendMessage` method will be used to tell the mediator passed in an argument what the message of the current `concreteUser` is. The `receiveMessage` method will be raised when the mediator broadcasts the message to all users.

Then, in the `User.swift` file, we implement our protocol, as shown:

```
class User: UserProtocol {
   var name: String

   init(name: String){
    self.name = name
   }

   func sendMessage(mediator:MediatorProtocol, message:AnyObject){
     mediator.broadcastMessage(self, message: message as AnyObject)
   }

   func receiveMessage(message:AnyObject){
     print("\(self.name) received \(String(message))")
   }
}
```

Here, we add an argument in the constructor to pass the name of the user.

In the `sendMessage` method, we see that we are calling the `broadcastMessage` method of the mediator passed in the argument.

When raised, the `receiveMessage` method will display the name of the current user and also the message that was received.

Next, lets see how `MediatorProtocol` is defined:

```
protocol MediatorProtocol {
   var users:[UserProtocol]? { get }

   func broadcastMessage(sender:UserProtocol, message:AnyObject)
   func register(users: UserProtocol)
}
```

The `MediatorProtocol` manages the collection of elements; here, it is `Users`. It can also broadcast a particular message to a user.

To add a user to the collection of users managed by the mediator, we add a `Register` method.

Let's see how we have implemented all of this in the `Mediator.swift` file:

```
class Mediator: MediatorProtocol {
    private let queue = dispatch_queue_create("MediatorPattern",
    DISPATCH_QUEUE_CONCURRENT)
    var users:[UserProtocol]? = [User]()

    func broadcastMessage(sender:UserProtocol, message:AnyObject){
      dispatch_barrier_sync(self.queue, { () in

        guard let users = self.users else {
          return
        }

        for u in users{
          if u as! User !== sender as! User {
            u.receiveMessage(message)
          }
        }

      })
    }
    func register(user: UserProtocol){
      dispatch_barrier_sync(self.queue, { () in
        users?.append(user)
      })
    }
}
```

First, we initialize a `User` array that is ready to manage a collection of user.

In the `register` method, we receive a user argument, which is added to the collection managed by the mediator.

Then, the `broadcastMessage` method:

```
guard let users = users else {
    return
}
```

We need to make sure that the user array has not a `nil` value, if this is the case we then do nothing by leaving the method invoking the `return` keyword.

Then, we iterate over all the users in the collection and if the current user of the iteration is different from the user sending the message (sender), then we call the `receiveMessage` method of the current user, along with the message to be transmitted.

**Concurrency protection**

You probably have seen the following line:

```
private let queue =
dispatch_queue_create("MediatorPattern",
DISPATCH_QUEUE_CONCURRENT)
```

We need to create concurrency protection in this pattern when various users try to access the same user at the same time, so we use a technology developed by Apple: Grand Central Dispatch which allow specific tasks in a program that can be run in parallel to be queued up for execution and, depending on availability of processing resources, scheduling them to execute on any of the available processor cores.

With this line, we initialize `queue` as a concurrent queue using `dispatch_queue_create`. The first parameter simply describes what our queue is (it could be helpful when you are debugging your code) and the second parameter specifies that we want our queue to be concurrent.

Next, we want to protect the access to our code where arrays are read and written. For this, GCD provides an elegant solution of creating read/ write lock using dispatch barrier. So we use `dispatch_barrier_sync` to pass our queue and the statement to execute by the queue. Since, the code we have written is a barrier closure, this will never run simultaneously with any other closure in queue . To see more about Grand Central Dispatch : http://www.raywenderlich.com/79149/grand-central-dispatch-tutorial-swift-part-1

All our participants are now in place. We will now try all of this in the `main.swift` file. We create four users, each with a name:

```
var user1 = User(name: "Julien")
var user2 = User(name: "Helmi")
var user3 = User(name: "Adrien")
var user4 = User(name: "Raphael")
```

Then, we instantiate our first mediator and add the first three users we have just created to the collection of users managed by `mediator1`:

```
var mediator1 = Mediator()
```

```
mediator1.register(user1)
mediator1.register(user2)
mediator1.register(user3)
```

Now, we want to test that `user1` can send a message to `user2` and `user3`. We only need to invoke the `sendMessage` method of `user1` passing the `mediator1` and the message to be sent:

```
user1.sendMessage(mediator1, message: "message1 from
    \(user1.name)")
```

So, in this case only `user2` (Helmi) and `user3` (Adrien) should receive the message from `user1` (Julien).

We want to try the pattern with another mediator but with only two users: `user2` and `user4`:

```
var mediator2 = Mediator()
mediator2.register(user2)
mediator2.register(user4)

user2.sendMessage(mediator2, message: "message 2 from
    \(user2.name)")
```

Here, only `user4` (Raphael) should receive the message from `user2` (Helmi).

Build and run the project. You should now be able to see the following result in the console dialog:

```
Helmi received message1 from Julien
Adrien received message1 from Julien
Raphael received message 2 from Helmi
Program ended with exit code: 0
```

# The observer pattern

The observer pattern is another behavioral pattern that is often used in networked system where a subject (the server) will notify some client. The iOS makes large use of this pattern through `NSNotificationCenter` object.

# Roles

The observer pattern creates dependence between a subject and observer so that the observer is notified in order to update their state each time the subject is modified.

This composition means that observer does not need to ask the current state of the subject. They only need to register to its notifications.

This pattern can be used when:

- A state modification inside the object needs to update other objects dynamically

- An object wants to prevent other objects without the need to know the type (without having to be high coupled with them)

- We do not want to merge two objects into one

# Design

The following diagram represents the UML class diagram of the observer pattern:

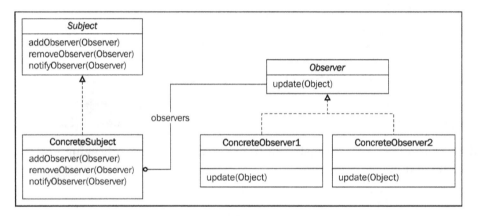

# Participants

This pattern is composed of the following participants:

- `Subject`: This defines the methods needed to add, remove, and notify observers.

- `ConcreteSubject`: This implements the `Subject` methods. It sends a notification when its state is modified.

- `Observer`: This is a common interface having an `update()` method, which will be invoked by the subject when the observer needs to be notified about the modification of the subject.

- `ConcreteObserver1` and `ConcreteObserver2`: This implements the `update()` method.

# Collaboration

The ConcreteSubject class notifies the observers when its internal state is modified. When a concrete observer receives this notification, it is updated consequently. To complete the update, it can invoke some subject methods that give access to its state.

# Illustration

You are working on a new website where you want to allow internet users to communicate each other through a chat system. Your first job will be to provide a room, the entry point of all Internet users. Each time a new user joins the room, every user is notified.

The observer pattern is fully appropriated to implement the code, which solves this problem.

# Implementation

Open the ObserverPattern Xcode project to see the current structure of our code:

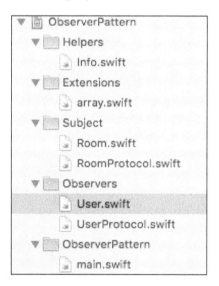

We will retrieve the Subject folder and Observers folder, where we will find the participants of our pattern. The Helpers folder contains a class that we will use later when sending a message.

The Extension folder contains an array extension that is required to make it possible for us to remove a particular object from the collection of users managed by the subject.

Lastly, we find the `main.swift` file used to simulate interactions.

So, let us begin our code by defining our observer in the `UserProtocol.Swift` file:

```
protocol UserProtocol {
    func update(object:AnyObject)
}
```

We simply define an update method with an object as an argument. The implementation of the `UserProtocol` will be like this:

```
class User: UserProtocol{
    let name: String!

    init(name: String) {
        self.name = name
    }

    func update(object:AnyObject) {
        let info = object as! Info
        print("\(self.name) notified that \(info.message) have status
        \(info.status) on \(info.date.description)")
    }
}
```

We pass a name in the constructor of the `User` object.

Then, in the `update` method, we prepare a message that will be displayed on the console. We downcast our object of type `AnyObject` to an `Info` object; this object is a helper. You will find its code in the `Helper` folder in the `Info.swift` file:

```
class Info {
    var date = NSDate()
    var message:String!
    var status:InfoStatus!

    init(msg: String, status:InfoStatus) {
        self.message = msg
        self.status = status
    }
}
```

The `Info` object contains three values: a date, message, and status.

The date is the current date and is defined when the `Info` object is initialized. The message is a string received in argument during initialization of the info object and the status is an enumeration passed in an argument during the initialization of the object and it can have the following value:

```
enum InfoStatus {
  case Join
  case Leave
}
```

Now, we only have to define our Subject protocol, and implement it in our concrete Subject. The Subject represents the object that need to be observed.

Our Subject definition is available in the `RoomProtocol.swift` file in the `Subject` folder:

```
protocol RoomProtocol {
  func addObserver(user: User)
  func removeObserver(user: User)
  func notifyObserver(object: AnyObject)
}
```

These three methods are the minimum necessary to any subject in an observer pattern.

The `addObserver` function lets you register an observer in the collection of observers managed by the subject.

The `removeObserver` method is used to remove an observer from the collection managed by the subject.

Last, the `notifyObserver` method is used to notify all our observers.

The implementation will be found in the `Room.swift` file, as shown:

```
class Room: RoomProtocol {

  private var users = [User]()

  func addObserver(user: User) {
    users.append(user)
    let info = Info(msg: "\(user.name)", status: .Join)
    notifyObserver(info)
  }

  func removeObserver(user: User) {
```

```
        users.removeObject(user)
        let info = Info(msg: "\(user.name)", status: .Leave)
        notifyObserver(info)
    }

    func notifyObserver(object: AnyObject){
        for u in users {
            u.update(object)
        }
    }
}
```

Here, you retrieve the three methods, in the two first one; you see a call to the notifyObserver method.

All the users will be notified each time the addObserver or removeObserver method is called because the addObserver method is called when a new user joins the room and we display the Join status in the Info message. With the same principle, we display the Leave status when the removeObserver method is called.

The notifiyObserver method receives an object of type AnyObject as an argument that will be propagated over the update method of each user object available in the collection managed by the Room method.

Time for us to now write our demo code, open the main.swift file, and write the code.

First, we initialize our Room method and four internet users:

```
let room = Room()
let user1 = User(name:"Julien")
let user2 = User(name:"Alain")
let user3 = User(name:"Helmi")
let user4 = User(name:"Raphael")
```

Then, we register each user to the room:

```
room.addObserver(user1)
room.addObserver(user2)
room.addObserver(user3)
room.addObserver(user4)
```

Each time the addObserver method is called, all the currently registered users will be notified that the current registered user has joined.

So, when room.addObserver(user1) is called, only user1 will be notified, but when user2 is registered, user1 and user2 will be notified and so on.

Now, we remove user2, user3, and user1 in this order:

```
room.removeObserver(user2)
room.removeObserver(user3)
room.removeObserver(user1)
```

To complete our sample, we register user2 once more:

```
room.addObserver(user2)
```

Let us now build and run the project. You will get the following result:

```
Julien notified that Julien have status Join on 2015-09-13 19:56:54 +0000
Julien notified that Alain have status Join on 2015-09-13 19:56:54 +0000
Alain notified that Alain have status Join on 2015-09-13 19:56:54 +0000
Julien notified that Helmi have status Join on 2015-09-13 19:56:54 +0000
Alain notified that Helmi have status Join on 2015-09-13 19:56:54 +0000
Helmi notified that Helmi have status Join on 2015-09-13 19:56:54 +0000
Julien notified that Raphael have status Join on 2015-09-13 19:56:54 +0000
Alain notified that Raphael have status Join on 2015-09-13 19:56:54 +0000
Helmi notified that Raphael have status Join on 2015-09-13 19:56:54 +0000
Raphael notified that Raphael have status Join on 2015-09-13 19:56:54 +0000
Julien notified that Alain have status Leave on 2015-09-13 19:56:54 +0000
Helmi notified that Alain have status Leave on 2015-09-13 19:56:54 +0000
Raphael notified that Alain have status Leave on 2015-09-13 19:56:54 +0000
Julien notified that Helmi have status Leave on 2015-09-13 19:56:54 +0000
Raphael notified that Helmi have status Leave on 2015-09-13 19:56:54 +0000
Raphael notified that Julien have status Leave on 2015-09-13 19:56:54 +0000
Raphael notified that Alain have status Join on 2015-09-13 19:56:54 +0000
Alain notified that Alain have status Join on 2015-09-13 19:56:54 +0000
Program ended with exit code: 0
```

Here, we see all the notifications. The first line corresponds to the first addObserver called. The next two lines correspond to the second addObserver called, and so on.

# Summary

A comparison between the mediator pattern and the observer pattern shows some of the similarities and differences. Both patterns facilitate the communication between the objects and both decouple the link between the sender and the receiver. The main difference is that in the mediator pattern, there is a notion of the participants and they communicate with each other using the mediator as a central hub, whereas in the observer pattern, there is a clear distinction between the sender and the receiver, and the receiver merely listens to the changes in the sender.

The communication in the mediator pattern is easier to understand. Elements send messages to a mediator and the transmission of the information further to whoever is currently in the group is handled there, in one place.

In the observer pattern, observers wait to be invoked with information from more than one subject. The coupling is closer in the mediator than in the observer.

This concludes this chapter. In the last chapter, we will talk about the last three behavioral patterns the: visitor pattern, the interpreter pattern, and the memento pattern.

# 8

# Behavioral Patterns – Visitor, Interpreter, and Memento

In this chapter, we will complete our discovery trip of the 23 Gang of Four patterns. Now, let's have a look at the three last design patterns of the behavioral patterns category. They are as follows:

- The visitor pattern
- The interpreter pattern
- The memento pattern

## The visitor pattern

In this section, we will talk about the visitor pattern, which allows us to separate data and their associated treatments.

## Roles

The visitor pattern allows us to externalize and centralize the actions that must be executed on object; these objects cannot have any links between them.

These actions will not be implemented in the class of the objects but in external classes.

So, this allows us to add any action in an external class, even a concrete visitor that implements **IVisitor**.

This pattern can be used when:

- We need to add functionalities to a group of classes without weighing down these classes
- A group of classes have a fixed structure and we need to add some functionalities to them without modifying their interface

The visitor pattern must be applied and used when you need to perform operations on objects of a collection that do not share a common base class or conform to a common protocol.

# Design

The following diagram shows us how objects and treatments are separated. Treatments are implemented in the ConcreteVisitor classes. The objects are implemented in the ConcreteElement classes, as shown in the following figure:

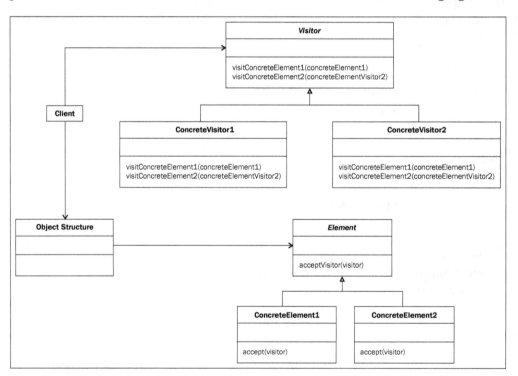

# Participants

The following are the visitor pattern participants:

- `Visitor`: This interface introduces the signature of the methods that realize a functionality in a group of classes. There is one method per class that receives an instance of this class as an argument.

- `ConcreteVisitors`: This implements methods that realize the functionality that correspond to the classes. This functionality is distributed in different elements.

- `Element`: This is an abstract class of the concrete elements class. It introduces the `accept(visitor)` method.

- `ConcreteElements`: This implements the `accept()` method, which consists of calling the visitor through the method that corresponds to the class.

# Collaboration

A client that uses a visitor needs to create an instance of a visitor in the class of its choice and then pass it as an argument to the accept method of a group of elements.

The element then calls the the visitor method that corresponds to its class. A reference to itself is sent back to the visitor that allows it to access its internal structure.

# Illustration

We are a car seller having three brands: DS, Renault, and Citroen, and each of them has a price.

We want to be able to modify the price without modifying our car concrete classes. For this, we will introduce our visitor pattern.

# Implementation

For this last chapter, we will use Playground. Now, open the `VisitorPattern.playground` file and let's have a look at how this works.

Here, we will use a technique called **Double Dispatch** that will allow us to perform the appropriate actions depending on the type of the object . This technique also help us to avoid making some type casting to perform the appropriated operation. (see the following URL to get more information: `https://en.wikipedia.org/wiki/Double_dispatch` if you need more informations about this technique)

First, we define our visitor protocol. The visitor has three visit methods having a `ConcreteElement` as an argument to accept each car type, as shown:

```
protocol CarVisitor {
  func visit(car: DSCar)
  func visit(car: RenaultCar)
  func visit(car: CitroenCar)
}
```

Then, we define our `Car` protocol. A car can accept a concrete `CarVisitor` object:

```
protocol Car {
  func accept(visitor: CarVisitor)
}
```

We can easily implement our three concrete cars. Each of them has a default price and also the `accept` method having a concrete `Visitor` object as an argument:

```
class DSCar: Car {
  var price = 29000.0
  func accept(visitor: CarVisitor) { visitor.visit(self) }
}
class RenaultCar: Car {
  var price = 17000.0
  func accept(visitor: CarVisitor) { visitor.visit(self) }
}
class CitroenCar: Car {
  var price = 19000.0
  func accept(visitor: CarVisitor) { visitor.visit(self) }
}
```

> The `accept` method defined by the `Car` protocol and implemented by the classes is the key to the double dispatch technique. By sending `self` as argument to the `visitor.visit` method, where visitor is our concrete visitor implementation of `CarVisitor`, Swift will choose the version of the `visit` method with the most specific type.

Lastly, we must implement our concrete visitor, our visitor is in charge of modifying the price of the `Element` class. The `Element` class modification depends on the type of object passed in the argument.

The DS car will see its price modified by 20 percent and the price of Renault and Citroen cars modified by 10 percent:

```
class PriceVisitor: CarVisitor {
  var price = 0.0
```

```
    func visit(car: DSCar)   { price = car.price * 0.8  }
    func visit(car: RenaultCar) { price = car.price * 0.9 }
    func visit(car: CitroenCar)   { price = car.price * 0.9 }
}
```

The client will be simulated with the following code. We will first instantiate our three car objects and add them in a Car array. Then we will define a new variable price, which is an array containing our three new prices.

For this, we will use the map function that is an extension of the array type. It allows us to execute a treatment on each element of the array. Here we can (for each element) instantiate a PriceVisitor object and pass it in the accept method of the current car object.

Then we return the new visitor.price, which is the new price of the current car object.

Like I said in the *Roles* section of this pattern, the visitor pattern is used when an array manages a heterogeneous collection of objects that does not share a common base class or conforms to a common protocol. By applying the pattern, all three Cars classes can share and conform to the same protocol and allow us to manage the following array:

```
let cars: [Car] = [DSCar(), RenaultCar(), CitroenCar()]
```

Then, we can calculate new prices by applying the appropriate visitor calculation:

```
let prices = cars.map { (car: Car) -> Double in
  let visitor = PriceVisitor()
  car.accept(visitor)
  return visitor.price
}
```

To show the result, check the right part of the following screenshot. **23200**, **15300** and **17100** are the new prices of our cars:

```
let prices = cars.map { (car: Car) -> Double in        [23 200, 15 300, 17 100]
  let visitor = PriceVisitor()                         (3 times)
  car.accept(visitor)
  return visitor.price                                 (3 times)
}
```

# The interpreter pattern

The interpreter pattern is not really used, but it can be really useful. Usually, this pattern is described in terms of formal grammar but the area where it can be applied, can be extended.

You can refer to the following for more information: Lecture de chiffre Romain (`http://www.oodesign.com/interpreter-pattern.html`) and `https://en.wikipedia.org/wiki/Roman_numerals`.

# Roles

The interpreter pattern defines an object representation of a language grammar in order to evaluate some expression written in this language by interpreting them.

This pattern can be used to interpret some expressions that are represented as a hierarchical tree. It may be applied when:

- Grammar of expression is simple
- Evaluation doesn't need to be quick

Some examples where this pattern can be used are:

- In rule engines
- To add some functionality to the composite pattern

# Design

The implementation of this pattern is seen in the use of the composite pattern applied to represent a grammar (refer to the *The composite pattern* in *Chapter 3, Structural Patterns – Composite and Flyweight*). The difference is that the interpreter pattern defines the behavior while the composite defines only the structure.

The UML class diagram of the pattern is as follows:

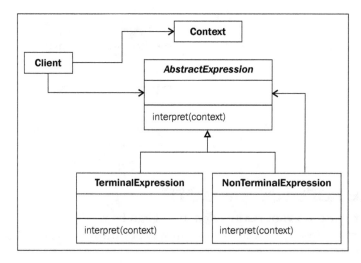

# Participants

Participants to this pattern are as follows:

- `AbstractExpression`: This defines the `interpret()` method that is common to all the nodes in the abstract syntax tree.

- `TerminalExpression`: This implements the interpret method associated with terminal symbols of the grammar. Each terminal symbol of the grammar requires a concrete class.

- `NonTerminalExpression`: This implements the interpret method and can also contain other `AbstractExpression` instances.

- `Context`: This contains information that is global to the interpreter. For example, the actual values of variables.

- `Client`: This builds an abstract syntax tree that is assembled from instances of `NonTerminalExpression` and `TerminalExpression`. It will be our demo usage of the pattern.

# Collaboration

The client builds the abstract syntax tree, initializes the context of the interpreter, and then invokes the interpret method.

The interpret method at the `TerminalExpression` and `NonTerminalExpression` node uses the context to store and access the state of the interpreter.

# Illustration

We want to create a roman number converter; you know the ones that interpret that XIV means 14 in decimals. The main purpose of our example is to write a roman number and our converter will tell us the decimal value.

# Implementation

Open the `InterpreterPattern.xcodeproj` file and see how we have implemented the pattern.

 For this pattern, all the code has been added to the `main.swift` class so that it can be easily exported into Playground if you want to see the live execution of the code.

Before starting to understand the code, have a look at the following link to understand how roman numbers work and how they are written.

You can see some rules about the roman numerals and also a roman numeral chart at `http://4thgradecrocs.weebly.com/roman-numerals.html` and how the roman system works can be seen at `https://en.wikipedia.org/wiki/Roman_numerals`.

For the pattern, we will use one string extension that lets us do a substring easily just by passing the number of characters we want to ignore in the argument:

```swift
extension String {
  func subStringFrom(pos: Int) -> String {
    var substr = ""
    let start = self.startIndex.advancedBy(pos)
    let end = self.endIndex
    let range = start..<end
    substr = self[range]
    return substr
  }
}
```

The expression to be interpreted is a string that is put in the context:

```swift
class Context {
  var input: String!
  var output: Int = 0

  init(input: String){
    self.input = input
  }
}
```

This class will help us to work while we apply the pattern; it consists of the remaining unparsed roman numeral strings and also the result of the numerals that are already parsed.

The context is passed to one of four sub-interpreters based on the type of interpreting (thousand, hundred, ten, and one). In this example, only `TerminalExpressions` are used.

Next, we will define our `AbstractExpression` class. This class must implement the `interpret()` method and define the methods that will be overridden in the subclasses:

```swift
class Expression {
  func interpret(context: Context) {
```

```
      if context.input.characters.count == 0 {
        return
      }

      if context.input.hasPrefix(nine()){
        context.output = context.output + (9 * multiplier())
        context.input = context.input.subStringFrom(2)
      } else  if context.input.hasPrefix(four()){
        context.output = context.output + (4 * multiplier())
        context.input = context.input.subStringFrom(2)
      } else  if context.input.hasPrefix(five()){
        context.output = context.output + (5 * multiplier())
        context.input = context.input.subStringFrom(1)
      }

      while context.input.hasPrefix(one()) {
        context.output = context.output + (1 * multiplier())
        context.input = context.input.subStringFrom(1)
      }
    }

    func one() -> String {
      fatalError("this method must be implemented in a subclass")
    }

    func four() -> String {
        fatalError("this method must be implemented in a subclass")
    }

    func five() -> String {
        fatalError("this method must be implemented in a subclass")
    }
    func nine() -> String {
        fatalError("this method must be implemented in a subclass")
    }
    func multiplier() -> Int {
        fatalError("this method must be implemented in a subclass")
    }
  }
}
```

The Expression class consists of the interpret method, which receives the context. Based on the current object, it uses specific values for thousand, hundred, ten, one, and also a specific multiplier.

The `one()`, `four()`, `five()`, `nine()`, and `multiplier()` methods of the `Expression` class are abstract. They will be implemented in our Concrete `TerminalExpressions` class

We can now implement our four `TerminalExpression` classes. Each of them override the `one()`, `four()`, `five()`, `nine()` and the `multiplier()` methods. These methods will then be interpreted depending on if we are in a thousand, hundred, ten or one expressions. Indeed, these classes are used to define each specific expression. Usually, these classes implement the `interpret` method, but here it is already defined in the base expression class and each of the `TerminalExpression` class defines its behavior by implementing the abstract methods: `one()`, `four()`, `five()`, `nine()`, and `multiplier()`. This is a template method (refer to the *The template method* section in *Chapter 5, Behavioral Patterns – Strategy, State, and Template Method*):

```
class ThousandExpression: Expression {
  override func one() -> String {
    return "M"
  }
  override func four() -> String {
    return " "
  }
  override func five() -> String {
    return " "
  }
  override func nine() -> String {
    return " "
  }
  override func multiplier() -> Int {
    return 1000
  }
}

class HundredExpression: Expression {
  override func one() -> String {
    return "C"
  }
  override func four() -> String {
    return "CD"
  }
  override func five() -> String {
    return "D"
  }
  override func nine() -> String {
```

```
      return "CM"
    }
    override func multiplier() -> Int {
      return 100
    }
}

class TenExpression: Expression {
    override func one() -> String {
      return "X"
    }
    override func four() -> String {
      return "XL"
    }
    override func five() -> String {
      return "L"
    }
    override func nine() -> String {
      return "XC"
    }
    override func multiplier() -> Int {
      return 10
    }
}

class OneExpression: Expression {
    override func one() -> String {
      return "I"
    }
    override func four() -> String {
      return "IV"
    }
    override func five() -> String {
      return "V"
    }
    override func nine() -> String {
      return "IX"
    }
    override func multiplier() -> Int {
      return 1
    }
}
```

The pattern is now written; we only have to test it. Before writing our test code, we will create a helper RomanToDecimalConverter() class having a calculate() method that returns the result of the conversion:

```
class RomanToDecimalConverter {
  var tree = [ThousandExpression(), HundredExpression(),
  TenExpression(),OneExpression()]

  func calculate(romanString: String) -> Int {
    let context = Context(input: romanString)
    for t in tree {
      t.interpret(context)
    }
    return context.output
  }
}
```

This class is responsible to build the syntax tree representing our specific value; the roman number, in the language defined by the grammar.

Note that we can only add our terminal expressions to the array in a specific order: from thousand to one expression, as we will parse the roman string from left to right.

We call the interpret method after the syntax tree is build. We return the context. output value once all expressions of the pattern are executed, which corresponds to the decimal result.

We will add a new method to our RomanToDecimalConverter before writing our test code. This will validate that the roman number that we are trying to convert is correct: otherwise, a message will be displayed informing us that our number is not a roman number. The added code is highlighted in the following:

```
enum FormatError: ErrorType {
  case RomanNumberFormatError
}

//Helper
class RomanToDecimalConverter {
  static let pattern =
  "^M{0,4}(CM|CD|D?C{0,3})(XC|XL|L?X{0,3})(IX|IV|V?I{0,3})$"
  let validation = NSPredicate(format: "SELF MATCHES %@",
  pattern)

  var tree = [ThousandExpression(), HundredExpression(),
  TenExpression(),OneExpression()]
```

```swift
func calculate(romanString: String) throws -> Int {
  guard validate(romanString) else {
    throw FormatError.RomanNumberFormatError
  }

  let context = Context(input: romanString)
  for t in tree {
    t.interpret(context)
  }
  return context.output
}

func validate(romanString: String) -> Bool {
  return validation.evaluateWithObject(romanString)
}
}
```

We first define a new `enum` function that we call `FormatError` of type `ErrorType`. We will use this to throw an exception when the format of the roman number is incorrect.

Then we have a static string `pattern` in the `RomanToDecimalConverter` class that contains our regular expression and also an instance constant called `validation` that will handle the validation process through an `NSPredicate` object. The purpose of this object is to define the logical conditions needed to constrain a search either for a fetch or for an in-memory filtering.

In the `calculate` method, we had a `guard` statement that executed the `validate` function, if the `validate` function returns `false` (meaning the number is incorrect), a `FormatError.RomanNumberFormatError` exception is raised; otherwise, we will continue the operation and calculate the decimal value using the pattern. Note the addition of the `throws` keyword just before the return type of the method. It means that this method can throw errors.

The `validate()` method calls the `evaluateWithObject` method of the `NSPredicate` instance by passing the roman number in an argument. This method returns `true` if the format is correct, otherwise it will return `false`.

The regex expression used in this code comes from the following URL and is very well explained at: http://stackoverflow.com/questions/267399/how-do-you-match-only-valid-roman-numerals-with-a-regular-expression

For more information about NSPredicate, you can refer to this site: https://realm.io/news/nspredicate-cheatsheet/

Now we can write our test code like the following:

```
let romanNumberToTest = ["XIV", "MCCMXXVIII","MCMXXVIII"]
var converter = RomanToDecimalConverter()
for roman in romanNumberToTest {
  var decimal = try? converter.calculate(roman)
  guard (decimal != nil) else {
    print("\(roman) is not a correct roman number")
    continue
  }
  print(decimal!)
}
```

We initialize an array with some roman numbers and then initialize our `RomanToDecimalConverter` converter object and loop over all elements to make the calculations.

We are using the following statement:

```
var decimal = try? converter.calculate(roman)
```

The decimal will return `nil` if an exception is raised. So, the next three lines help us to print an appropriate message when a roman number doesn't have the correct format.

With the three values of our array and after building and running the project, you'll obtain the following result:

```
14
MCCMXXVIII is not a correct roman number
1928
Program ended with exit code: 0



All Output ◇                                              🗑 ▯▭▯
```

The preceding result given by the program inform us that **MCCMXXVIII** has a wrong roman number format and the two others numbers are well converted with the 14 decimal value for the first roman number and 1928 for the second roman number.

You can try running the code using the roman numeral chart given at the beginning of this section.

You can see that this pattern is really interesting. You have already seen that the composite and template method patterns have also been used to build and implement our interpreter pattern with our use case.

# The memento pattern

The memento pattern will be the last pattern that we will discover together. You will see that this pattern is really interesting to work with and has many uses.

## Roles

The role of the memento pattern is to capture an object's internal state and save it externally so that it can be restored later without breaking the encapsulation of this object.

## Design

The generic UML class diagram is defined as the following:

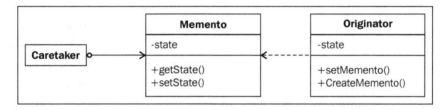

## Participants

The following are the participants of the memento pattern:

- Memento: This is the class for the objects that saved the internal states of origin objects (or part of this state), such as the introduction of the fact that the saving of a state can be made independent of the object itself. The memento has two interfaces:
  - A complete interface for Originator objects that permit access to everything that needs to be saved or restored
  - A narrow interface to the caretaker that can keep and pass on the memento references, but no more

- Originator: This is the object class that creates memento to save their internal states and that they can restore from memento.

- caretaker: This is responsible to manage the list of mementos and doesn't provide access to the internal state of the origin objects. This is also the class that the client code needs to access.

- `CreateMemento`: This method is used to save the state of the originator. It creates a `Memento` object by saving the state variable into the `Memento` object and returns it. This is used to record the state of `Originator`.

- `SetMemento`: This class stores the historical information of the `Originator` objects. The information is stored in its state variable.

# Collaboration

An instance of `Caretaker` asks for a memento of the `originator` object by calling the `createMemento` method and saves it. In case of cancellation and going back to the saved state in the memento, you can send it to the `originator` object using the `setMemento` method.

# Illustration

You have developed a platform game where each time your hero passes a level, a checkpoint is stored. This allows the player to reload from any level that he has already crossed.

The data that needs to be stored when saving the checkpoint are the level numbers, the current weapon, and the number of points.

# Implementation

To simplify our code, we will use an OS X command line project, where we will write all our code in the `main.swift` file.

Open the `MementoPattern.xcodeproj` file in Xcode and let's see how we have organized our code.

Firstly, we define our `GameState` structure: data that needs to be saved are `level`, `weapon`, and `points`:

```
struct GameState {
  var level: Int
  var weapon: String
  var points: Int
}
```

Then we define our `Originator` with the `createMemento` and `setMemento` methods:

```
protocol Originator {
  func createMemento() -> GameMemento  func setMemento(memento:
GameMemento)
}
```

Then we implement our `GameState Memento`: it contains all the information that `CheckPoint` needs to restore the state.

First, we define three variables that will help us to store states:

*   `entries` is a list of `GameState`
*   `nextId` contains the next index of the `entries` array
*   `totalPoints` is a variable that has the total points of each entry

We have a constructor where we can pass a `CheckPoint` object as an argument. States of the checkpoint are assigned to the memento internal variables.

The `apply()` method receives a checkpoint object in the argument. Then, we assign the current memento values to the checkpoint properties in order to restore the checkpoint state:

```
struct GameMemento {
  private let entries: [Int: GameState]
  private let nextId: Int
  private let totalPoints: Int

  init(checkPoint: CheckPoint){
    self.entries = checkPoint.entries
    self.nextId = checkPoint.nextId
    self.totalPoints = checkPoint.totalPoints
  }

  func apply(checkPoint: CheckPoint) {
    print("Restoring a game state to a checkpoint...")
    checkPoint.nextId = nextId
    checkPoint.totalPoints = totalPoints
    checkPoint.entries = entries
  }
}
```

We can now save and restore a memento. The next thing to be done is to create our originator: the `CheckPoint` object. While playing the game, an entry will be added to the checkpoint entries list.

Just like in the `Memento` object, we will define three variables. The difference being that we initialize them in this object:

- `Entries`: This is an array that will contain all entries.
- `totalPoints`: This is an integer initialized to `0` and it will contain the total of each level points.
- `nextId`: This is an integer that starts from `0`. It contains the value of the next index in the `entries` array.

We have four methods:

- `addGameStateEntry`: This method is used to add a new entry to our entries list. This will be called by the client every time a level of our game is complete.
- `createMemento`: This method creates and return a memento object. The checkpoint itself is sent as an argument of the method.
- `setMemento`: This method allows us to restore a `Memento` object.
- `printCheckPoint`: This method is here to easily see what the current state of the `CheckPoint` object is.

The `CheckPoint` class has the following implementation:

```
class CheckPoint: Originator {
  private var entries: [Int: GameState] = [:]
  private var totalPoints: Int  = 0
  private var nextId: Int = 0

  func addGameStateEntry(level: Int, weapon: String, points: Int)
  {
    let entry = GameState(level: level, weapon: weapon, points:
    points)
    entries[nextId++] = entry
    totalPoints += points
  }

  func createMemento() -> GameMemento {
    return GameMemento(checkPoint: self)
  }

  func setMemento(memento: GameMemento) {
```

```
        memento.apply(self)
    }

   func printCheckPoint() {
      print("Printing checkPoint....")
      entries.sort {$0.0 < $1.0 }
  .map {
          print("Level: \($0.1.level)   Weapon: \($0.1.weapon)
          Points: \($0.1.points) ")
      }
      print("Total Points: \(totalPoints)\n")
    }
}
```

You have probably seen the following statement:

```
      entries.sort {$0.0 < $1.0 }
  .map {
          print("Level: \($0.1.level)   Weapon: \($0.1.weapon)
          Points: \($0.1.points) ")
      }
```

This is how we can easily sort our array by index value. Then we can use the map function, only to be able to execute the print statement on each entry of the array.

You can see more information about closures to the following URL at: https://developer.apple.com/library/prerelease/ios/documentation/Swift/Conceptual/Swift_Programming_Language/Closures.html

Our pattern is now in place, let's have a look at how to use it:

```
let checkPoint = CheckPoint()
checkPoint.addGameStateEntry(0, weapon: "gun", points: 1200)
checkPoint.addGameStateEntry(1, weapon: "tommy gun", points: 2250)
checkPoint.printCheckPoint()

let memento = checkPoint.createMemento()
checkPoint.addGameStateEntry(2, weapon: "bazooka", points: 2400)
checkPoint.addGameStateEntry(4, weapon: "knife", points: 3000)
checkPoint.printCheckPoint()

checkPoint.setMemento(memento)
checkPoint.printCheckPoint()
```

After initializing a checkpoint object, we add two entries to the checkpoint.

After calling the printCheckPoint method of the checkpoint object: we obtain the following result:

```
Printing checkPoint....
Level: 0   Weapon: gun    Points: 1200
Level: 1   Weapon: tommy gun    Points: 2250
Total Points: 3450
```

The printCheckPoint method iterates over all the entries of the checkpoint object and displays the state of each one and the total points of the entries.

At this moment, we have still not created a Memento object, so we cannot restore a previous state.

To create a memento, we only have to call the createMemento method of the Originator object (in our case the checkPoint object):

```
let memento = checkPoint.createMemento()
```

This method returns a memento object that we assign to our memento constant, so that we can restore when needed.

We continue the game and pass two others levels successfully and print the current checkpoint state once more:

```
checkPoint.addGameStateEntry(2, weapon: "bazooka", points: 2400)
checkPoint.addGameStateEntry(4, weapon: "knife", points: 3000)
checkPoint.printCheckPoint()
```

The result is as follows:

```
Printing checkPoint....
Level: 0   Weapon: gun    Points: 1200
Level: 1   Weapon: tommy gun    Points: 2250
Level: 2   Weapon: bazooka    Points: 2400
Level: 4   Weapon: knife    Points: 3000
Total Points: 8850
```

The CheckPoint now contains four entries in its array.

We want to restore our checkpoint state to the last saved state. To proceed, we only need to call the `setMemento()` method of the checkpoint object with the memento object we previously have created and make a call to the `printCheckPoint` method to display the result, as shown:

```
checkPoint.setMemento(memento)
checkPoint.printCheckPoint()
```

The result of the `printCheckPoint` call is the following:

```
Restoring a game state to a checkpoint...
Printing checkPoint....
Level: 0   Weapon: gun    Points: 1200
Level: 1   Weapon: tommy gun   Points: 2250
Total Points: 3450
```

We can see that the checkpoint object has been restored to its previous state.

With this simple example, you should now have a good pattern to use and easily manage cancellation and restoration of an object.

The memento pattern is a pattern that is extensively used in scientific computing to save the state of long-running computations. As seen here, it may be used to save the state of play over a matter of hours or days. In the graphics toolkit, it may be used to preserve the state of a display while the objects are being moved around.

Use this pattern when:
- An object's state must be saved to be restored later
- It's undesirable to expose the state directly

# Comparing the three patterns

Though they seem dissimilar, there are several ways in which we can compare these three patterns:

- **Reusability**: All three patterns aim to relieve the developer of implementing a common code repeatedly. Indeed, once the visitor has been implemented, they can be reused with different types of objects without any changes. To facilitate the reuse, you must limit the number of states the visitor needs to be aware of. The interpreter pattern is designed to parse an input where the structure is data driven. The `Caretaker` and memento classes of the `Memento` pattern are independent of the data, only the originator should be changed.

- **Working with structure**: These patterns are intended to work with structures. Visitor and interpreter require the developer to write traversing codes whereas the memento pattern moves the structure as a whole, relying on the serialization to do the traversing.
- **Objects as argument**: In the memento and visitor patterns, objects are passed around as a part of their structure, while in the interpreter pattern it relies on a context that is basically the evolving state of the input that is being interpreted to output.

# Summary

This chapter concludes the discovery of the eight behavioral patterns, as described by the gang of four. Moreover, this chapter concludes the book.

I wanted the book to be really easy to follow without adding complexity in the sample provided. This book is intended to be a reference for anyone who wants to implement design patterns with Swift.

There are some points that we have not covered, such as multi-concurrency access, Swift 2 special coding with closure, and so on. I think that these points don't occur in a learning book. The main purpose of the book is to easily find the appropriate pattern when needed and have an easy illustration to follow.

Well, you now have all the necessary information to structure your code in a scalable way. This will help you to structure your code properly, increase the performance of your code, and reduce maintenance costs.

I really thank you to have followed the book. Now, it's up to you to put this knowledge into practice.

# Index

**Thank you for buying**
# Swift 2 Design Patterns

## About Packt Publishing

Packt, pronounced 'packed', published its first book, *Mastering phpMyAdmin for Effective MySQL Management*, in April 2004, and subsequently continued to specialize in publishing highly focused books on specific technologies and solutions.

Our books and publications share the experiences of your fellow IT professionals in adapting and customizing today's systems, applications, and frameworks. Our solution-based books give you the knowledge and power to customize the software and technologies you're using to get the job done. Packt books are more specific and less general than the IT books you have seen in the past. Our unique business model allows us to bring you more focused information, giving you more of what you need to know, and less of what you don't.

Packt is a modern yet unique publishing company that focuses on producing quality, cutting-edge books for communities of developers, administrators, and newbies alike. For more information, please visit our website at www.packtpub.com.

## About Packt Open Source

In 2010, Packt launched two new brands, Packt Open Source and Packt Enterprise, in order to continue its focus on specialization. This book is part of the Packt Open Source brand, home to books published on software built around open source licenses, and offering information to anybody from advanced developers to budding web designers. The Open Source brand also runs Packt's Open Source Royalty Scheme, by which Packt gives a royalty to each open source project about whose software a book is sold.

## Writing for Packt

We welcome all inquiries from people who are interested in authoring. Book proposals should be sent to author@packtpub.com. If your book idea is still at an early stage and you would like to discuss it first before writing a formal book proposal, then please contact us; one of our commissioning editors will get in touch with you.

We're not just looking for published authors; if you have strong technical skills but no writing experience, our experienced editors can help you develop a writing career, or simply get some additional reward for your expertise.

## Learning Swift

ISBN: 978-1-78439-250-5          Paperback: 266 pages

Build a solid foundation in Swift to develop smart and robust iOS and OS X applications

1. Practically write expressive, understandable, and maintainable Swift code.

2. Discover and optimize the features of Swift to write cleaner and better code.

3. This is a step-by-step guide full of practical examples to create efficient IOS applications.

## Mastering Swift

ISBN: 978-1-78439-215-4          Paperback: 358 pages

Master Apple's new Swift programming language by following the best practices to write efficient and powerful code

1. Start with basic language features and progressively move to more advanced features.

2. Learn to use Xcode's new Playground feature as you work through the immense number of examples in the book.

3. Learn what makes development with Swift so exiting and also get pointers on pitfalls to avoid.

Please check **www.PacktPub.com** for information on our titles